THE ATYPICAL LEADER

Harnessing the Power of Neurodiversity

Twenty-two leadership lessons from a senior executive who started off in the class for 'slow learners' on his journey to the boardroom of a Fortune 5 company

By Rick Brennan

Dedication

To my children—I'm so proud of who you've become—and to all those who have taught, inspired, and tolerated me through the years

We all make mistakes, have struggles, and even regret things in our past. But you are not your mistakes, you are not your struggles, and you are here NOW with the power to shape your day and your future.

Steve Maraboli

Author, *Life, the Truth, and Being Free*

Standard definition

Atypical

[cy-**tip**-i-kuhl]

Not typical; not conforming to the type; irregular; abnormal.

"A flower atypical of the species."

> exceptional
>
> singular
>
> deviant
>
> unorthodox
>
> out of the ordinary
>
> unique

Atypical leader

An individual who is 'rarely associated with leadership positions.'[1]

Innovator from the margins.

My expanded definition

The people I describe as 'atypical' are those (like myself) who have struggled with countless limitations and challenges throughout their lives. This has caused them to see life and business through a different lens, developing skills and a perspective unique to them that are different from the norm.

CONTENTS

Foreword 8

Discovering my atypical self 12

Your childhood doesn't define you 19

22 ATYPICAL LEADERSHIP LESSONS 27

LESSON 1

Be brave 28

LESSON 2

Sometimes learning hurts 35

LESSON 3

Starting to believe in me 39

LESSON 4

I knew I wasn't intelligent, so I got smart! 46

LESSON 5

Listen, learn, and adapt, but never lose yourself in the process 61

LESSON 6

Smart people accept help 67

LESSON 7

Half of leadership is just being organized 78

LESSON 8

Be bold and prepared to take crap for doing the right thing 83

LESSON 9

Take the time to understand your limitations 87

LESSON 10

Mix business and personal as often as you can! 94

LESSON 11

Leave enough room for the possibility that you don't know shit 104

LESSON 12

Find leadership experiences outside of work 115

LESSON 13

Create an environment where you can shine 131

LESSON 14

Make everyone accountable, including you! 146

LESSON 15

Look for what others don't see 161

LESSON 16

Live your entire life like there is no box 173

LESSON 17

Done is better than perfect *184*

LESSON 18

I tried, but I just couldn't stop learning! *195*

LESSON 19

Never compromise who you are *208*

LESSON 20

The Leadership Façade *220*

LESSON 21

Don't lose yourself in the madness *228*

LESSON 22

Understanding the atypical leader's headspace *237*

FINAL REFLECTIONS 247

BONUS: HOW TO GET STARTED 252

REFERENCES 261

Foreword

I believe that Rick Brennan's life is an example of business leadership expert Price Pritchett's saying: "If you must doubt something, doubt your limits."

Our brains are full of stereotypes and prejudices. The models that business presents to us of what a leader should be like simply fulfill those stereotypes. Thousands of articles and books on leadership are published every year, but none quite like this one.

I adhere to the concept that a leader transcends the limits of a given structure. Our genetics define the tools we have to work with, but two people with a similar genetic profile can build very different lives, making what they can achieve unpredictable.

According to Michael Shinagel, former Continuing Education Dean at Harvard Extension, "Leadership is an art, not a science. And leadership is not limited to a professional field or industry. Leaders transcend the confines of a defining box."

This book should be required reading at all levels of education, especially in business schools—first and foremost to help all of those who feel inferior when classic leadership parameters are measured. But it should also reach all of the executives and managers who will undoubtedly have people on their teams who don't fit the mold but with a little help are capable of rising above everyone's expectations.

I have had the great pleasure of being Rick's executive coach for a considerable period of time. As part of the coaching process, I analyzed his personality tests. Therefore, I was aware of his supposed 'limitations' as a leader. But I also saw what made him special.

Rick possesses outstanding listening, understanding, and execution skills. I remember he used to put every analysis, comment, and new perspective that I showed him into practice between sessions. Nothing ever stayed in theory; it was always about how to put recently acquired knowledge into practice.

As a leader, it is very important to differentiate between aptitudes, attitudes, and values. Rick excelled at this. His awareness of his supposed limitations gave him a higher-than-average score on empathy; in his eyes, everyone could do better if they put their minds to it. And isn't it the essence of leadership to guide people toward becoming the best version of themselves?

How did Rick do it? He knew perfectly well that our environment exerts a very powerful influence on us, and we tend to define ourselves through how the environment defines us.

But there is another way, Rick's way: Stand up for who you are, celebrate your uniqueness, and don't let the environment define you.

When you read Rick's book, you'll be amazed by his level of self-awareness, insight, and analysis. Whatever he was doing in his life, Rick was always able to distill from each experience important lessons about the principles and stereotypes of leadership. It is fascinating to see how he learned from the world of kids' sports, extracting very powerful teachings applicable to the world of business.

Rick's concrete business results and the recognition he has received from the members of his team are the best way to understand leadership. He is understood by his impact, not by his theories. After all, leadership is about results, and that has been Rick's focus. In his own words, "done is better than perfect."

I believe this book should open a new path in the identification of potential leaders for any organization. Job interviews *per se* are never definitive, and personality tests are helpful, but which personal traits guarantee success? There is no way that the types of abilities that made Rick successful would be evident in a typical job interview.

One lesson you will surely learn from this book is that leading people is an art, and different people can cultivate it in very different ways.

Our perspective determines how we see the world and the people in it. Without a doubt, Rick did not meet the traditional expectations for a Senior Vice President at a Fortune 5 company like McKesson. However, key people in the organization were able to see past those limitations and understand what Rick could bring to the table. And they were not wrong!

Ultimately, Rick used his strengths to offset his challenges. His strong presence and his ability to establish alliances and inspire others were remarkable. He didn't check the boxes of the standard profile of a successful executive, and yet, he invariably outpaced most.

Rick's unique skills were enhanced by the way he managed his so-called 'disabilities.' In fact, he was able to understand that his perceived limitations were the doorway to his superpowers.

I am elated that Rick has decided to go public and tell his story. I believe that this book will be an invaluable asset for those dealing with challenges similar to the ones that Rick faced and for anyone searching for the secret of successful leadership.

Sorry, my friend, but you don't have the right to settle down yet.

Dr. Carlos Davidovich, MD
European Mentoring and Coaching Council
Global Executive Coach
Neuromanagement Professor
Author and Consultant

Discovering my atypical self

When I was well into a successful career, my oldest brother said to me, "You know, we always worried about what would happen to little Ricky." Apparently, I had lived my entire life oblivious to the fact that I was the front runner for being crowned as the family's most likely member to self-destruct.

It was shocking to find out my family was worried that I'd amount to nothing as an adult. Fortunately, by the time I heard those words from my brother's mouth, I had already proved them wrong.

I was nine years old when I first found myself in the class for slow kids. Without any diagnosed or visible disabilities, I felt embarrassed, hurt, and betrayed. Almost immediately, the so-called normal kids started acting weird; teachers suddenly expected less of me (I'd get a gold star for sharpening my pencil), and even my own family seemed to look at me differently.

I wondered, *what have I done wrong?* I knew I wasn't the most intelligent kid in class, but in my young mind, I didn't connect doing poorly in school with being different or 'slow.' Yet, this new assessment of who I was changed everything, and it made me feel like I was some sort of 'failure in waiting.'

That was who I was at the start of my life's journey—a little boy filled with negativity, feelings of inferiority, and self-doubt. Over the next chapter of my life, I'd live up to these expectations, acting horribly, disrespecting everyone and everything, and getting into all kinds of trouble with the help of drugs, booze, and partying—the whole ball of wax. Adding to my glowing resume, I continued to do poorly in school regardless of how much teachers dumbed things down.

People like me rarely advance through the corporate ranks. By most accounts, I was a below-average guy—impatient, stubborn, and pigheaded. Many would go so far as to call me an asshole.

I never had any of the traditional leadership skills that companies tend to look for. My scores on Myers-Briggs, Pathfinder, and all those silly psychological tests sent red flags flying. I spent a lifetime focused on having fun, finding others who wanted to have fun, breaking rules, and getting in and out of trouble. I had to cheat my way through school to pass. I couldn't write a clear sentence. I struggled with authority, ADHD, dyslexia, dyscalculia, OCD, cognitive dysfunction, and anxiety. I was plagued by repetitive thinking that was agonizing and often kept me awake at night. It's an endless list of faults and limitations.

Yet here I am, recently retired from a job running the largest group of independent pharmacies in Canada—2,500 stores doing billions in sales for a Fortune 5 company—and responsible for building and operating a world-class shared services organization while earning some of the highest employee engagement scores in the world. During the COVID-19 pandemic, I was called on to join Canada's National COVID Task Force for Critical Drugs.

When I wasn't working, I was coaching. The teams I coached won seven provincial titles in two different sports, and I led five teams to the Atlantic Championships in five consecutive years.

You may be asking yourself, *How did someone with seemingly so little to offer achieve so much?* God knows I do.

Over the years, I have had hundreds of people under my supervision. I am as bold and brash as it gets and always focused on reaching my objectives. As a boss, I was demanding and never had a problem telling subordinates the brutal truth about their performance.

When the news broke about my retirement, I started receiving letters from people I had worked with over the years. I was baffled by what they were saying and how they remembered me. Suddenly, people I thought I was tough on were coming out of the woodwork to tell me I had a "huge positive effect on [their] 38-year career" and that I had been the "best coach and mentor" they had ever known. The author of those words, Troy Ferguson, was a guy I hadn't spoken to in twenty years.

"You challenged me, pissed me off, told me the truth, and provided a great deal of guidance and leadership. Most of all, you believed in me, which shaped and molded me into the person I am today," Troy wrote. *"I am in recruitment now and have been for almost ten years. I feel I have had a great career (five years to go, fingers crossed) and wanted to share this with you. It's important to me that you know how many people's lives you affected in such a positive way back in Halifax so many years ago. Thanks for that!"*

It was this and similar messages that started me on an introspective journey that would culminate in the writing of this book. I had so many questions. If I was so flawed, so inappropriate, and wild at times, how had I not only been successful but also influenced others in such a positive way?

Perhaps another person could have taken the praise, said thanks, and moved on, but I was too intrigued; I had to know more.

Among the many notes I received, one from Scott Barron stood out. I was Scott's boss for seven years, but we hadn't spoken in a long time. We had seldom seen eye to eye, which led us to lock horns and fight it out on occasion. I didn't have him pinned down as one of my biggest fans—far from it.

"You taught me a lot over my years," Scott wrote after stumbling on me at a conference. *"You were always open with me and never held back the truth that ultimately would help me be better. Most people have trouble telling the whole truth to their employees, and that does not help them grow... There have been many times over the past few years that I have said or done something and said to myself, 'That was from the Rick Brennan school.'"*

The letter that had the biggest impact on me was written by a former assistant of mine by the name of Melanie Landry. It bore some clues about what it was I did differently as a leader and shone a light that would help me discover what I could contribute to the world as a retiree.

According to Melanie, I had helped her overcome her "insecurity and lack of confidence.... *Having you as a boss has given me back my confidence and love for work. You believed in me, trusted me, and were always honest and straightforward. They say every person you meet on your journey is for a reason, and it's true. You were put on mine to give* me confidence and self-respect, and to overcome the fear of not being perfect."

Melanie's letter quoted me as saying, *"I don't want you to be perfect. You are who you are; you have all the right pieces. It makes you you, and that's perfect!"*

That was the key to solving the puzzle. It seems that despite my imperfections and my rough and rowdy ways, people saw something in me that helped them embrace their true selves.

As I reflected on all the messages I received, I realized that people didn't give a shit about the mistakes or missteps, and our disagreements were long forgotten. Even our victories and successes seemed almost irrelevant. More than anything, they valued openness and straightforwardness. They cared because I cared; they put a high value on trust and respect because I did. Still, it was hard for me to comprehend the impact I seemed to have on others. Sure, the messages made me feel good, but they also made me feel awkward and uncomfortable.

In an attempt to understand what was happening, I talked to my VP of HR, Melita, who said, "I'm not surprised by people's positive remarks and the reason you're feeling uncomfortable. Well, my friend, that's called humility." Then, she recommended I listen to "Captain's Class—7 Core Qualities of True Leaders," a podcast based on a study by Sam Walker. "It's your style all the way, and it should help you in understanding why so many see you as a leader!"

Walker examined the personal characteristics of the leaders of the most successful sports teams in history. While I assumed these great leaders would have been the captain or coach, charismatic, polished, enamored with the spotlight, great motivational speakers, and probably the best players on the team in their athletic years, they were none of those things. They were confident but reserved, undiplomatic yet humble, practical, and hardworking. They avoided the spotlight and were rarely the stars of any teams. Their success and, ultimately, the team's success came from an unselfish approach to leadership. They were totally focused on the collective goals that superseded any need for individual accomplishments.

As I listened to the podcast, I realized that Melita was right. What Sam Walker called 'functional leadership' faithfully mirrored my operating style and my approach to teamwork. In my case, it came about more by accident than by design. I just wanted to win, and I knew I was incapable of doing it alone and that my best chance for success was with a group of like-minded, motivated people. It seemed like a no-brainer.

Yet, it was still unclear how I evolved from a troubled kid into this person who seemingly impacted so many lives in positive ways. Looking for more answers, I talked to my brothers about our family history and their impression of me as a child. Their comments made me realize how much impact the events of my early years had on how I saw myself and how others saw me.

I was a mess growing up—a couple of wrong turns away from living under an overpass or being thrown off one. Yet, despite these seemingly insurmountable obstacles, after I got out into the real world, things slowly started to fall into place. I became a successful business executive and a confident person with many good and trusting friends. This was much more than the outside world had led me to believe I was capable of achieving.

Perhaps there was more to me than just a problem child with learning disabilities. I even dared to think that maybe I had never been a 'failure in waiting' but a 'leader in hiding.'

This book is about that discovery. I have written these pages for everyone who has ever felt the way I have: defeated before you got started because you were labelled as 'different,' defined by what you couldn't do, and characterized by your worst moments.

I am here to tell you that it's all nonsense; *your uniqueness is your power*. My journey is proof that your atypical traits can be tamed and mastered, giving you the wisdom and perspective to see and do things that others can't.

I want to take you on an emotional journey from my early years as a screwed-up kid to an undisciplined and disrespectful young adult, party animal, corporate rebel, and, ultimately, a successful Fortune 5 executive.

I want to show you how I turned my limitations into superpowers and inspire you to do the same—because if I could do it, so can you.

Your childhood doesn't define you

To understand how I came to embrace my uniqueness and discover my hidden talents, you have to understand how I was shaped (but not defined!) by my childhood. I think of myself as proudly atypical now, but that was not always the case.

The first place I can remember living was St-Hubert, Quebec, an Air Force base just outside of Montreal and across the border from New York, where my father was stationed for ten years. My father was a Sergeant in the Canadian Air Force, a well-liked guy who provided for his family and worked multiple jobs while always finding the time for a little fun.

My mother was a loving woman, devoted to her children. She cooked our meals and took care of all the domestic chores. Raising seven kids was her mission in life, and with the kids ranging in age from post-university to newborn, her hands were full. My oldest sister, Patsy, was the star of the family and the one most like my mother. I don't know how she did it, but none of us were ever wanting for my mom's attention.

My parents were 'common folk' with modest aspirations who made the personal sacrifices needed to ensure their kids had the basics. They appeared satisfied with their station in life. Being the sixth of seven children, I missed most of the tough years when they just got by. They were married for twenty years with five kids before they even owned a car! Whatever the economic situation, I loved those early years in St-

Hubert; it was the first place I called home. It's where I had my first group of friends; I was part of the 'in' crowd.

Living on the base was a self-contained world, with pools, gyms, grocery stores, and schools; the outside world was almost unknown to us in those early years. Hell, the other side of the base was unknown to us.

I lived at 30 Pine Circle. The park was just down the street, the woods were right behind our house, and that's where we hung. My family lived on one side of a duplex, and my best friend, Richard, and the Pelland family lived on the other side. Richard and I were best buds, always together. He was big and strong and the best at everything; man, he was so cool, and because I was his best friend, I was cool by association.

I have so many great memories from those days: receiving my toy M16 rifle "with real live sound" that I just had to have (I cried for weeks before my parents finally caved), breaking my arm as I flew out of a toboggan (almost killing myself), drop-kicking a twenty-foot telephone pole, throwing a tomato through a church window, hanging with my dog Sam. All the good stuff!

That was also when I had my first girlfriend, Sandra Fontaine, who was tall, blonde, and beautiful, which complemented my short, skinny, goofy look. We were only eight years old at the time but deeply in love. Well, until it went beyond passing notes in class. The moment I had to speak to her face to face was the very moment our love's eternal flame fizzled out.

Saturday nights were special for us Brennan boys. My father, my brother Paul, and I would watch Hockey Night in Canada and the Montreal Canadians. My Dad would bake frozen fried chicken in the oven, and the smell would fill the house. To this day, anytime I hear the Hockey Night in Canada theme song, I smell that fried chicken.

As the years in St-Hubert went by, I progressed through elementary school, gaining weight and confidence. I even had the opportunity to pick on a few kids—not that I am proud of it now, but that is what I saw others doing, so I thought I'd give it a try.

Once, I was giving a kid a hard time on a school outing. He was so terrified of me, I thought he was going to shit his pants. So, naturally, being the colossal dick that I was, I chased him down, cornered him, and commenced to beat him down. The 'fight' was broken up when a teacher ran over and pulled us apart. Knowing damn well I had started the scuffle, he scolded me. Looking me right in the eye, he said, "Ricky, get a life," which really struck a chord in me.

His words made me feel so stupid, guilty, and ashamed. That moment alone put an end to my 'tough guy' ways.

Aside from that small error in judgment, life was rolling along pretty well. That was until tragedy struck our family.

One summer night, my sister Patsy was at a friend's and wanted to stay the night. She was leaving for Florida the next day, so my mother demanded that she come home. I went to bed before Patsy returned.

The next morning, I came downstairs to find a living room full of women. They appeared to be comforting my mother, who was crying. Without much introduction, she announced to me that Patsy was gone.

On a whim, I replied, "I know" (everyone knew she was going to Florida). I had no clue what was going on. Why was mom crying, and why were all these women in my house?

I then went directly outside and played in the dirt, not sure what to do or how to act, until my friend Richard came to my rescue and explained, to my dismay, what was going on. After that, it's all a blur.

Years later, I would piece the story together. Patsy was riding in a car with friends. Along the way, they stopped to help a driver who was having car trouble when a drunk driver hit their car with five people inside. Patsy was killed; none of the others were seriously injured.

I didn't go to the funeral; I'm not sure why. They must have thought I was too young to understand, unable to grasp the magnitude of our loss. I remember riding my bike around the church, asking my father if my buddies and I could go in and see the casket. We did, and then off we went.

This tragedy and its aftermath would change my life forever. While I am not sure about my dad, I don't think my mother ever really recovered from my sister's death. The last conversation she had with Patsy was an argument. If Patsy had stayed over at her friend's place, she might still be alive today. The grief of Patsy's death devastated my mother, and the decision to make her come home that fateful night would haunt her for a lifetime.

This tragedy sent my family into shambles. My mother was emotionally detached, both of my parents had an infant to take care of, my siblings were older and dealing with the loss in their own ways, and then there was little old me, blowing in the wind, left to figure it out on my own.

My parents, brothers, and sisters never talked about Patsy's death, and it would be this silence, this feeling of walking on eggshells, that made me feel abandoned and confused. The trauma, the silence around what had happened, and the new family dynamic rattled me—not so much on the outside (I didn't cry, act out, or misbehave) but hidden deep inside for nobody to see. That was until I began to suffer from what I called 'day-mares,' which I assume we would call panic attacks today. I would be sitting in class, wide awake, and at any given moment, I would experience these nightmare-type episodes. As a result, I failed grade four and was then banished to the class for 'slow kids' the following year.

My mother had blind faith in the wisdom of authority. So, when the teachers said I was slow, that meant I was! When a friend of hers (a captain's wife or someone who she thought was smart) confirmed my issues and validated my predetermined path in life, it confirmed in her mind that I was indeed troubled and doomed.

I was just a kid when all this happened, and I didn't realize the significance of these events. I knew my sister's death was sad, but I didn't get why no one was talking about it. I didn't understand the complexity of the trauma that my family and I were experiencing. I instinctively knew my family cared about my well-being, but they were wounded, my mother was lost, and none of them seemed to be in a position to help me.

All I know is that Patsy's death, and more importantly, the aftermath of her death, left me seeing myself as stupid and unbalanced, instilling in me a negative self-image that I would grapple with for decades to come.

There are many success stories about people who struggled in their youth but had someone who pointed them in the right direction—a teacher, a mentor. That was not my story. My mother was a very different person after my sister's death, and there was no one stepping forward to save my soul.

I was left blowing in the wind with zero emotional support except my friends, who were kids themselves. No hero magically appeared on the horizon to see my potential and steer me down the right path.

To make matters worse, soon after my sister's death, my father decided to retire, uprooting me from the home I knew and the friends I loved, the two connections I needed most at the time. From a very early age, I had to figure it out on my own.

The events related in this chapter taught me many things—first and foremost that your childhood doesn't define you, and you should not let other people define you. The good intentions of people, even those who love you, can't determine your future or predict the wonders that may lie within you.

My mother loved me dearly, but her personal trauma, coupled with my being labelled as 'slow,' made her think of me as a kid with limited prospects. Meanwhile, her submission to authority figures probably triggered the opposite in me. As my career progressed, my irreverence toward authority was obvious to everyone. This was often a stumbling block to my progression, yet it gave me the space to develop an unfiltered perspective of people and events, which would be at the core of who I was to become.

The power of friendship is something I understood early on, thanks to my connection with my friend Richard. He made me believe I was cool and smart. I am sure he never said that directly, but he sure made me feel that way. As time passed and I moved away, I would on occasion return to St-Hubert to see my friend, and no matter how shitty things were at home or how much I was being bullied, when I arrived in St-Hubert, I instantly felt cool and accepted. Crazy same old me, but when the environment changed, I felt and reacted differently.

When I returned to my new home in Chatham, New Brunswick, all my insecurities returned, and I acted and felt like the people in Chatham defined me, or maybe more accurately, I *thought* they defined me. Even when I return to Chatham today and attend a sporting or social event where I see loads of people from the past who are actually very nice to me, I get the same 'not up to par' feeling in my belly. This seems to validate the notion that we are all a product of our environments.

I would later learn, however, that my perception of what others thought or did rarely had anything to do with me. It's astonishing to me now that I wasted so much time worrying about things I couldn't control. The false narrative I created in my mind caused me so much stress, stifled so many relationships, and made me appear to be so arrogant and standoffish. One piece of advice I would give my younger self and those reading this book would be, 'live life in the moment.' Spend no time second-guessing what other people might think, say, or do.

This difficult period in my life also taught me to value friendship, be trustworthy, and formulate my own opinions based on facts and information that I collected from people I trusted. I also learned to not believe rumour, old wives' tales, or the pitch of the day, regardless of how well people spin their tales.

22 ATYPICAL LEADERSHIP LESSONS

LESSON 1

Be brave

Better to embrace the discomfort of being different than the comfort of fitting in.

Ogwo David Emenike

In 1969, my father decided to take his pension from the Air Force and move the family back to his hometown of Chatham, New Brunswick. Although it was in a different province and nearly eight hundred kilometers from St-Hubert, Chatham was a familiar place to me. We spent several weeks there every summer at our cottage overlooking the banks of the Miramichi River.

My father's brother and his family lived next door. Another uncle and his family lived in the old Brennan homestead next to them, and a herd of other uncles and cousins lived just minutes away. As a result, there always seemed to be some relative sitting at the kitchen table having a cup of tea.

My maternal grandmother, Nannie, lived up the road with my step-grandfather, Evie. He was a great guy and a bit of a lunatic. Evie loved to do two things: drive his moped and drink his Hermit Sherry. Unfortunately, he often combined his two passions.

You could usually find him with a big smile on his face, dead drunk, and speaking a language that no one could understand while on his way to find another drink. You'd see him from a mile away swerving along on his moped, wearing his fire truck-red helmet over his swollen red beak of a nose, guiding his way like an inebriated Rudolph.

When he got home, Nannie would take one look at him and start giving him hell, chasing him around the kitchen with a broom. My cousins and I would just sit there chuckling, and Evie would give us a wink and a smile as he ran for his life.

My first summer after the move to Chatham was pretty normal. We swam and played down on the rocky beach below the house; climbed the big apple trees at the home of our neighbors, the Rubensteins (to Mr. Rubenstein's dismay); played in the cars at the local junkyard; and spent endless hours walking the railroad tracks with my dog Sam.

Sam was my best friend and consummate companion. He comforted me as I struggled with Patsy's death, the changing family dynamic, and the move to a new town.

Sam and I would frequently run around the neighborhood chasing one another and terrorizing the birds and squirrels. One afternoon when we were out doing some exploring, we were just about home when Sam, who had been trailing behind, stopped at the edge of the road across from my house. I commanded him to cross, and being the obedient dog he was, he ran across the road, only to be met head-on by a Chevy. He was killed instantly.

Some messed-up things can happen to a kid, but killing your dog (and only friend) and seeing it happen tops the list by a long shot. The guilt and shame I felt were crippling, and the loss of my little friend left a mountain-sized hole inside of me.

Soon after my puppy's demise, it was time to start school, where they were still trying to figure out if I was going into grade six or grade seven. Due to my failing grade four and being in the class for slow kids, there was some discussion about holding me back again. I'd badgered my parents all summer, and they felt sorry for me about Sam, so they agreed to let me go into grade seven.

Like any kid starting a new school, I didn't have it easy. I was coming from a military environment to a small town where they did things their way and where the cliques were already well established.

When I left St-Hubert, I felt like a cool kid who was part of the 'in' crowd. I would soon learn that without Richard by my side, I wasn't so cool after all, and I sure as hell wasn't part of the 'in' crowd. The bullying started almost immediately. Charley horses, slaps to the back of the head, intimidation, and name-calling were routine. They called me 'football' for a while. I wasn't sure why. Maybe because they kicked me around so much, or was it the shape of my head? I had no idea.

My general appearance didn't help much; I dressed like a redneck. My hair stuck out on one side, my ears were far too big for my head, and I had a mole on the side of my face with about an inch of hair growing out of it.

In an attempt to look a tad less pathetic, I grew out my hair, but then I would forget to wash it, so my strategy didn't help much. When I think back about my appearance, I can't help but wonder where the hell were my parents to give me a kick in the ass, some advice, some words of wisdom, shampoo, anything??

It wasn't until my older brother Carl, home on vacation, asked me, "Why the hell don't you cut the hair growing from the side of your face" and my cousin Helen told me to "try using shampoo" that I got the hint and cleaned up my act.

By the end of grade eight, I was worn down by bullies. Tired of being the butt of the joke, I did the only thing you could do back then to earn an ounce of respect. I fought back.

I carefully selected my opponent, Louis C. He was just the right amount of pipsqueak, incapable of causing me too much damage yet close enough to my size that I could still earn some respect around town for getting into the ring, win or lose.

Following some light banter—it didn't take much—we got off the bus and went at it. A pretty big crowd was cheering us on, which was fantastic for me because, for once, I was not only winning the fight but kicking his butt! Right or wrong, when you've dealt with rejection and bullying for a while, this is a pretty proud moment for a kid.

The fight ended abruptly when my extremely embarrassed mother came running out of the house, screaming, "What will the neighbours think?"

The next day, as proof of my victory, the side of Louis's face was black and blue, and I remember one of the cool kids telling me to give Louis a hard time. But for some reason, as much as I wanted to be a cool kid, I refused to do it. Maybe it was the memories of how I felt when that teacher scolded me back in St-Hubert or the bullying I was experiencing myself. I don't know; I just knew I couldn't do it.

The rest of the year would pass without incident, and the following year I was off to grade nine, where I would face a new lineup of kids for the first time, many of them coming from the military base.

Finding my crew

The class was fun, everyone got along, and I made some good friends. One of those friends was Danny Carroll—tall and skinny, a poor student like me, funny, and full of piss and vinegar. He didn't take crap from anyone.

Danny had a special way about him. He was capable of delivering the most unexpected remarks that would send the classroom, even the teacher, into uncontrollable laughter.

As the year progressed, our relationship would grow, and he helped me grow a backbone— well, kind of. He demanded that I stand up for myself, and, slowly, with his very direct encouragement, I would start to show traces of self-confidence.

I remember we were playing some type of game at the gym one afternoon, and some of the cool kids were trying to take over the court. Danny wasn't having any of it, and lo and behold, I jumped in to help. Now, Danny didn't think I jumped in quick enough, and he was probably right, but from where I was standing, I was an absolute beast! I may have only hung around with Danny for that school year, but he certainly had a positive impact on me and my feeling of self-worth, though he probably doesn't even remember today.

My best friend was Gary Farrah. He was an interesting guy. He got along with everyone—the rough crowd from the hill, the kids from the military base, the guys in the rock bands, and even the nerds in the chess club.

This was a quality I truly admired; I had such a hard time connecting with people from outside my direct circle of friends. Either I felt too shy and uncomfortable, or I thought they still saw me as that wimpy kid. I'm not sure, but it caused me a type of awkwardness around people that often came across as arrogance.

Gary and I shared our first experiences smoking grass as we tried hopelessly to get high, but with the combination of poor-quality marijuana and our inability to inhale, it took us almost a year to get it right.

The pot smoking that I started in junior high would become a big part of my life for decades to come. I became a different person when I smoked weed: funny, relaxed, creative, and confident, and it seemed to help counterbalance the nervousness I often felt.

As time went on, my friends would beg me to smoke more and drink less. I was just too out of control, too much of an idiot when I drank, and it seemed that smoking grass made me at least tolerable.

As a result of the friends I made in grade nine and Danny's clear instructions not to be such a chickenshit, grade nine would be a turnaround year for me. I felt ready for my next challenge: high school.

My brief time with Danny was a game-changer. He forced me to be brave; he believed in me and had no patience for my 'poor little guy' routine. It was 'stand up for yourself' with really no option but to do so. I can see now that I later projected the same sorts of demands on my team members as I tried to get them to be the best version of themselves.

I can't say I went through life thinking how profound Danny's actions were, but as I look back at that period, I begin to realize how the smallest interaction can have a profound impact on others. So, go out into the world and be positive and kind; you just never know when you might change someone else's life or your own.

Key takeaways

- Look for positive role models hidden in plain sight.
- Embrace your weirdness.

LESSON 2

Sometimes learning hurts

The longest journey is the journey inward.

Dag Hammarskjold

As I entered James M. Hill High School, I'd come a long way. I was still academically challenged and socially awkward, yet optimistic about my next few years. I made some new friends and even got myself a steady girlfriend, my first love, Karen Trear. She was a smart, mature girl with her head on straight who had a positive influence on me; I almost felt normal!

Nonetheless, after a year or so, she came to her senses and sent me on my way; man, it hurt! I'd soon recover, spending most of my time with 'the boys' on the shores of the Miramichi, hanging out downtown, or tilting back a few drafts at the Ambassador tavern.

In those days, it was pretty normal to get drunk and smoke a little weed on the weekends, and when I say drunk, I mean fall-on-your-face drunk. We drank a lot of warm beer, but our all-time beverage of choice was Hermit Sherry, just like Evie drank. The price was right at $1.45 a bottle. It tasted like sewer water but did the trick, which led to a lot of foolishness and a whole lot of kids getting sick.

Learning to keep my mouth shut

One fateful night, I was drunk, hanging out with my buddies in front of the bowling alley, when another crowd of kids showed up. The leader of the group was holding a bottle of booze in the air, and in my drunken wisdom and without provocation or reason, I grabbed the bottle from him.

Naturally, he took exception, and we got into a fight that ended with me on the losing end. Then, as insecure teens do, to protect my ego, I started running my mouth off like a chainsaw, telling anyone who would listen that if it happened again, I'd kick his ass, blah, blah, blah.

Well, my 'tough talk' got back to him, and he challenged me to another bout. That was the last thing I wanted. I was just acting tough, trying to reclaim a little of my lost pride.

Then, one night, I was walking into the local arena to watch a high school hockey game when I saw that he and his buddies were outside. When he saw me coming, he instantly made a beeline toward me and started swinging. As I was on the ground, one of his friends went to kick me in the head with all his force. I somehow managed to move my head, and he missed. Had he connected, I might be sucking my dinner through a straw even now!

The feud with this group of kids would go on for years. To them, I was public enemy number one. It was a pretty intimidating situation at times, and it would take my anxiety through the roof.

It was an ordeal brought about not by the original fight and me grabbing the bottle but by my need to shoot my mouth off and talk tough. Had I owned up to my responsibility for causing the altercation, the aftermath could have been avoided. I can't say I understood my actions at the time. They were likely caught somewhere between trying to act cool, showing people I wasn't such a wimp, misplaced confidence, and plain stupidity.

I'd like to say I learned a lesson from all this, but unfortunately, my errors in judgement would only accelerate. When alcohol was involved, my actions were totally reckless, pushing me from one predicament to another. Yet, this particular episode would stay lodged in the back of my mind for decades, and as time passed, I would come to realize how this encounter was instrumental in teaching me to control my actions and understand that every action has consequences.

It was an important lesson for me and for anyone to learn, especially for us quick-to-action, Type A's. As you go out into the world, be bold, but temper your actions, take a breath before reacting, and seek to understand before committing to a position.

I would continue to struggle academically. It was not that I couldn't concentrate or wanted to be somewhere else—nothing as cliché as that. I just didn't get it. Math, Chemistry, English—every subject seemed impossible. I couldn't understand the simplest concepts, and even when I knew the material, transferring that information to paper was an insurmountable task. I tried studying, but that only caused me to get more confused, with everything getting bungled up in my head.

I had no idea what was wrong with me. I just thought I wasn't as smart as the other kids. It became clear that if I had any chance in life, I'd have to find more creative ways to jump the hurdles that were piling up in front of me.

Finding my niche

As I struggled with coursework, my friend Terry Williston told me that the new town pool was looking for lifeguards and favoured hiring local kids if we could get the needed certifications. So, I donned my Speedos, and off we went.

I spent countless hours at the base pool, swimming laps and taking the various Red Cross swimming courses, where I was lucky enough to make some good friends. I did get the job as a lifeguard, which would make for a great summer job and, as a bonus, did wonders for my image.

Key takeaways

- Know that your actions may have unintended consequences.
- Let your brain catch up to your mouth.

LESSON 3

Starting to believe in me

Focus on your strengths instead of your weaknesses, on your power instead of your problems.

Paul Meyers

You could say that I discovered I could be a good leader by accident. I owe much of my success and my perspective on leadership to my experiences coaching sports teams. Being a coach taught me that winning involves equal parts hard work and sheer fun. I also learned that if you have a vision, you have to stick to it no matter what others say, especially the people running the circus. Nobody wins a championship by sticking to a manual or directives from above. Winning takes true passion and instilling enthusiasm in your team. As I have always done, I acquired this wisdom by doing rather than following someone else's lead.

From the bottom of the heap to a powerhouse

My first experience leading a team came as a natural follow-up to summertime lifeguarding. I started coaching the local swim team. We wouldn't have much success in the first few years; we were just too young and foolish. I don't think we even thought about winning.

As the years went by, I started getting more serious about coaching and more intrigued with the idea of winning, and we decided that our goal was to win the provincial championships. In 1977, we won our first provincial title by a whopping 250 points, an incredible achievement for those kids.

The next year, we were back at it, winning our second provincial championship by almost 500 points, a record that I'm sure still stands today. Somehow, whatever we did caused this ragtag group of kids to rise from the bottom of the heap to a powerhouse in two short years.

As you can see from this excerpt from the local newspaper, we were not on our rivals' radar:

"The Miramichi swim team, a group of 50 or so youngsters ranging from 8 to 17 from Chatham and Newcastle, were scheduled to compete in the provincial championships outdoor meet in Fredericton. Last weekend on the eve of the meet, the coach of the Fredericton team said in the Daily Gleaner, 'I'm expecting 20 to 25 clubs in the province. The competition should be close. The bigger clubs, Fredericton (oh, yes!), Moncton, St. Stephen, Campbellton, and Edmunston are all neck and neck. As it turned out, these teams did finish neck and neck, but only as they were bunched together, far behind the Miramichi team. Our team finished first with 761.5 points, with Fredericton, a very, very distant second at 284 points. This was a huge, two-day championship with 120 events and so many competitors that some of the events required eight heats before a winner could be declared. Nevertheless, our kids won it easily. The one thing that particularly infuriated me when I saw that piece in the Daily Gleaner was that the Chatham-Newcastle team had won the provincial title the previous year."

Later, local reporter Dave Butler wrote, "The Miramichi team's home base is about 100 ft from where I'm writing this, and I looked out of my den window all summer to watch the Miramichi team practicing. They worked hard for what they won, and I was glad to see them thrash the rest of the province. My heartiest congratulations to head coach Rick Brennan and assistants Ricky Daley, Robbie Malley, Suzanne McCarthy, Paul McKinnon, and Anne Gallant."

Making hard work and fun seem like the same thing

Dave was right. The kids worked their guts out for what they accomplished. Each one of them realized that hard work meant success, and quickly, the idea of 'giving it all you have' became a badge of honour.

There was, however, one other thing they loved more, and that was playing 'murderball.' At the end of every practice, we'd form two teams and go at it. The object was to get the ball from one side of the pool to the other. There were no rules; well, maybe you couldn't drown anyone. It was open season on the coaches, and they loved it. It was just good old-fashioned rough-and-tumble fun, and it seemed to strengthen us as a team.

The environment we created, almost by accident, where hard work and fun became the same thing, took the team's performance to a level that none of us could ever have imagined.

My instinct was always to have fun first. I viewed hard work as something to be avoided. But when my drive to accomplish a goal became important to me, the hard work became effortless. My enthusiasm just overpowered the idea that things were hard.

I had coached the swim team for a number of years before we even looked for success. As time passed and I connected with the kids, I couldn't help but want them to enjoy their experiences to the fullest.

When we began to enjoy minor success, that built my confidence (and theirs), and we agreed to refocus and chase the provincial title. Keep in mind that I was, at best, an average competitive swimmer, and my knowledge of specific swimming skills and training was limited. I only knew that if we wanted to win, we had to be in the best physical condition, and that meant hard work. But then, the kids started complaining about working so hard, so I gave them the carrot: "Work hard, and we'll do some fun things!" Murderball was always at the top of their list.

The formula worked. The idea of fun, our connection, made the idea of working hard easy, and over time, it was just the way we rolled.

The hard work was a little more complicated than that. I developed different training techniques that I knew the kids would like and have fun with. The result was astonishing: total domination. And the depth of the team was incredible; in some events, we took the top six spots.

My training techniques were very different from what the provincial swimming body was pushing, but I stuck to my guns and ignored their guidelines. After all, the kids liked it, their performances were improving, and their hard work blended into the fun perfectly.

Even then, it was clear that driving their enthusiasm and staying focused on teamwork was far more impactful on their performances than adhering to prescribed training techniques.

My interaction with the kids was incredibly rewarding. And even at my young age, I knew this experience would be one of the highlights of my life. I'd like to say that our success was the product of a masterful strategy I spent hours developing, but it was just me doing what I needed to do to win. That meant ensuring the kids got what they wanted: connection, fun, laughter, and a sense of pride and ownership.

I would apply the same philosophy later in my life with all of my teams. This was not because I reflected back on the swim team experience so much; it was just what came naturally to me. Of course, later in life, as I got older, my approach matured, yet I'd have to say it's pretty much the same at its core. In retrospect, the experiences with the swim team changed the way I saw myself. I started to realize that despite my countless shortcomings, my limitations didn't define me.

Rite of Passage No.

As high school came to a close, we all gathered to say our goodbyes. We were having a few drinks when someone blurted out the idea that we should paint 'Class of 75' on the wall that had just been built in the center of town.

To me, it was the greatest idea I'd ever heard, so I spirited home, grabbed a can of white paint, and off we went to etch ourselves into our high school history books.

Halfway through our composition, the owner came outside screaming, causing me to panic and paint the 5 in 75 backward. Just so we're clear, I didn't paint it backward, like 57. No, I wrote the 5 as you'd see it in a mirror.

The next day, our 'piece de resistance' was quite the sight! While we thought our work of art would make us legends, with the 5 backward, it only made us look like idiots.

To make matters worse, the next morning, the cops showed up at my door. Oh, no! What would the neighbours think? My parents were fuming, but as hardened criminals do, I stayed cool and denied everything.

Unfortunately, not everyone had the same gangster-esque composure; someone cracked, and we were forced to confess to our not-so-perfect crime. We ended up paying to have the wall cleaned, and they sent us on our way with a slap on the wrist.

When I reflect on that night so many years ago and the backward 5, I've come to realize that this 5 was a clue to my yet-to-be-recognized learning disabilities. But back then, it was just a drunken mistake by a dumb kid and something to laugh about. I headed off to university with limited expectations, simply looking for a good time and ready to take whatever came my way.

As I look back at my years with the swim team, I've come to realize what an incredible gift it was and how it created in my mind the vision of what a team could be. We were all just kids back then, yet this experience instilled in me the belief that a positive, fun-filled, relaxed environment was the key to success. Even back then, it wasn't easy staying in our happy bubble. I was consistently fighting with the provincial governing body, which was trying to make us conform to their standardized training methods. But my stubbornness wouldn't allow me to comply, so I told them what they wanted to hear and then did what I wanted.

In time, I would come to understand that what I thought was stubbornness on my part was me instinctively protecting my team and our environment from outside forces. I learned that the establishment writes the rules and then evaluates its success based on its ability to get people to comply. Even as we went on to dominate the province, winning by numbers that no one had ever seen before, the swimming establishment didn't reassess their directives, praise our actions, or explore the golden nuggets in our homegrown system. No, they criticized my actions and frowned on our success.

I knew that if I folded under the pressure, followed their directives, and acted like everyone else, success would be unlikely. So, be a maverick, stand up for your beliefs, and do what you believe is best for you and your team.

Key takeaways

- Hard work and fun must coexist.
- Consider other points of view and then do what *you* think is right.

LESSON 4

I knew I wasn't intelligent, so I got smart!

He who laughs most learns best.

John Cleese

As I entered pre-adulthood, I believed that anyone with even a hint of ambition should go to university. And if, by chance, I stank at it, I'd be doomed to the life of mediocrity that so many believed I was destined for anyway.

My path in life would challenge those views, but I still had so much to learn, and going through university would give me the freedom to push my boundaries and come to terms with the worst pieces of me.

Welcome to Party Central

Following my quick encounter with the law, it was finally time to leave the nest. I was off for my freshman year at Saint Thomas University (STU) in Fredericton, New Brunswick. The decision to attend STU was an easy one. They accepted my application, and nobody else did. Quite frankly, I considered it a miracle they let my slow-ass in.

I visited STU the previous year with a few of my buddies. We had the same mission as always: party and meet girls. We spent the weekend diligently trying to accomplish our goal. Considering that we'd been drinking at a high school level, this was like being called up to the majors directly from T-ball. We felt up to the challenge, though, and did our best to hold our own drinking with the guys from Harrington Hall and brutally had our egos checked striking out with college girls in the women's residence, Vanier Hall. We ended the night laughing our asses off after being kindly asked to leave by the very hot proctor on duty, Rachel. Needless to say, we had a ball and suddenly became ambitious scholars.

When I arrived in September 1975, it was Frosh Week—seven solid days of chaos and partying. I had never felt more at home. For most students, Frosh Week would be a huge hooray, and then they would ease into a more practical schedule, keeping the party alive on the weekends while staying afloat in classes during the week. I took a more 'poetic' approach to college. Frosh Week wasn't the climax; it merely set the pace. Thankfully, I quickly found a crew who shared my philosophy. The fun times never seemed to end. The year would be filled with nonsense: raids on Vanier Hall, drinking, smoking pot, hanging in pubs, and my favourite activity: heading over to Riverview Arms.

The Arms was an old tavern at the bottom of the hill just below the university. To put it frankly, it was a dump, but it was our dump—about as 'divey' as a dive bar could get before it's closed due to botulism. A draft beer was forty cents, and we'd buy them by the tray-full, guzzle them down, and spill more than we drank. By the end of each night, the floor would be covered with beer and broken glass. It was beautiful.

Our main mission was chasing girls; the drinking and smoking grass gave us our superpowers, aka 'fantastic personalities,' to summon our prey.

Oh, and remember Rachel, the proctor who kicked me out of Vanier Hall during my first visit? Well, I eventually managed to charm her into going on a date. I guess I had developed better negotiating skills by then.

During my time at Saint Thomas, I lived in Holy Cross House, which was a little unusual. Most partiers like me lived in Harrington Hall, which was Party Central. Holy Cross, on the other hand, mostly housed the older and more serious students, with many of the STU faculty (most of whom were priests) living on the third floor. With so many upperclassmen in Holy Cross, you'd think they would have been better role models, full of wisdom and good sense. But that was not the case.

Cheating to survive

As the year continued, the partying intensified, and the stories piled up. I was totally out of control at times. My outrageous behavior had a very polarizing effect on people, especially those on the receiving end of my fun.

Meanwhile, I continued to struggle academically, overwhelmed by the most basic concepts. Combined with my poor writing skills, this made getting passing grades almost impossible. I tried to study, but the more I studied, the more confused I got. Even when I knew the answers, I still seemed to do poorly on tests. It was the same old story; I either couldn't understand the questions being asked or I couldn't transfer what I knew to paper.

Cheating became the thing I had to do if I had any chance of passing. Crazy enough, even when I cheated, it didn't seem to help much. Due to my inability to write a clear sentence and explain my point of view, it seemed that nothing made sense to the reader.

I once managed to secure a copy of the Sociology midterm exam in advance. I carefully did my preparation and wrote the answers in the exam booklet. When I then sat for the exam, I handed the pre-completed booklet to the professor at just the right moment. Nobody was the wiser. This should have gotten me my first A, but it didn't. Even after having access to the exam in advance, with the answers at my fingertips, I received a C-.

I often wondered over the years if my cheating was okay. If I had not cheated, I would have never gotten the jobs I did or met the people who would positively influence my life. I most certainly would have never realized my potential, which seemed to be hidden deep inside.

In those days, there was no help for someone with learning issues, not even a recognition that we had them. You were just not smart, not up to standard, or plain stupid.

In today's world, if my kids ever cheated, I'd be so disappointed in them, but those rules, at those times, just didn't seem to apply to me. With the few skills I had, and with no help available, it was a matter of survival.

Hammering my way to rock bottom

As my first year was coming to an end, I decided to head out west to find a job for the summer. My destination was Brooks, Alberta, where my sister Gail lived with her husband, Jim, and their two kids.

My sister was a kind soul, but her husband Jim and I never saw eye to eye. He thought I was irresponsible and didn't understand my carefree approach to life. My cousin, Barry, and my friend, Peter, joined me, and we all got jobs on the same crew framing houses. We didn't have a clue what we were doing. Trevor, our boss, would show us the tricks of the trade, and off we went, hammer in hand!

Then, as crazy as it sounds, after three months of building experience, we started framing houses on our own. There was so much construction going on in Alberta at the time that it prompted builders to do stupid things, and trusting the likes of me was certainly one of them. Our main tools were a chainsaw and a sledgehammer. If a wall wasn't level or it didn't fit, we'd cut or bang the hell out of it until it did.

Sometimes we worked as part of a larger crew. On one occasion, we were building one side of a fourplex while a group of indigenous Canadians built the adjacent unit. They were a tough bunch. They loved to get drunk and fight with the locals, and every last one of them had been to prison at one point or another.

Late one Friday afternoon, both crews decided to head to the local tavern. In those days, there was bad blood between the local boys and the indigenous Canadians. So there we were, on one side of the bar with our First Nations friends and the locals on the other.

At one point, someone thought he heard one of the local boys make a comment he didn't like, and that was all it took. Without a moment's notice, the entire population of the bar was on its feet and swinging with their eyes closed. It was the type of scene I only thought was possible in

Clint Eastwood movies. Women were beating up men, women were fighting women, bar patrons were breaking bottles on the table to use as weapons, chairs were broken across people's backs. The only thing missing was a mustached piano man setting the tempo and a sheriff to bust through the door and fire his pistol into the ceiling.

I thought about joining in for a half-second, saw a guy get driven through a table headfirst, came to my senses, and ran away. It's fun to look back at it now, but we learned pretty quickly not to go out for drinks with that particular group of work buddies.

I did my summer thing in Brooks and then returned to school in Fredericton. I had a lot of fun there for about a month, and then I decided that school wasn't for me and made the big decision to head back to Brooks.

I got myself a job, and my brother-in-law, Jim, who was still trying to save my soul, got me a tryout with the local junior hockey team, the Brooks Lakeside Spurs. I managed to make the team, but I was definitely out of my league.

Partying was, of course, the first order of the day. Between hanging with the hockey guys, my roommates, and the local guys I met, I managed to party almost every night. I ended up leaving Brooks, knowing that if I kept up that pace, I'd probably be dead before my time.

The final straw was when I woke up one morning, passed out under the kitchen table clutching a kilo of grass, and hungover, with the dog we had just adopted sleeping on my chest. Within three days, I sold everything I owned, including my Pontiac Laurentian, which I let go for the steep price of $60, and a small bag of weed. I boarded a bus and headed home.

My experiences in Brooks changed my perspective on the value of schooling and gave me a different point of view on the type of jobs I might want in the future. I knew that, somehow, I would have to find a way to make school work for me.

I would return to Saint Thomas to finish my degree and, while there, I played both varsity hockey and soccer. The hockey team was like most sports teams, with the best player taking the leadership role. It seemed to be the natural thing to do. The leader's approach of 'live up to my standard,' however, only seemed to alienate and polarize many on the team. Well, at least it alienated me, and as a result, I had zero commitment to him or the team.

I remember getting hurt once and having to leave the game, but instead of staying and supporting my team, I left and got an early start at the pub. On another occasion, I forgot about an 'away' game and entered the cafeteria all 'stoned up' with two of my buddies (Tom and John) just as the hockey team was leaving. Let's just say our self-proclaimed leader wasn't very impressed. Sadly, I couldn't care less.

Sometimes rules need to be broken

Playing soccer was a different experience. It was a different group of guys with different values who collectively shared the leadership role. They all valued teammates' contributions regardless of talent. As a result, it was easy to be committed to each other and the team.

Of course, fun was the first order of business, with a very memorable trip to a tournament in Truro, Nova Scotia. We got through the tournament in good shape and were heading to the finals on Sunday.

Our coach was LeRoy Washburn, who was also the athletic director at the university—a good guy, a former Olympian, and a distant relative of mine. What I found interesting about LeRoy's coaching style was that despite his countless years of experience and success as an athlete, he felt no need to control. He knew his audience; he gave us advice and guidance and let us take it from there.

The evening before the finals, he gave us an eleven p.m. curfew. That seemed reasonable because we had the championship game the next day, but there was one problem: We were on a road trip, it was Saturday night, and it was party time! Like any hormone-fueled group of college-aged guys, we hit the bars the moment we could. We drank like we had won something already, we met some girls, and I ended up bringing a date back to the hotel.

When I got back with her on my arm, the first person I ran into in the lobby was LeRoy. Now, between the cross-eyed look on my face and the sheepish look of my lady friend, all LeRoy could do was shake his head and laugh. The rest of the team soon returned with dates of their own, and the craziness continued. To protect the reputation of all involved, we'll end the story there.

The next day, we were all a mess, but we pulled ourselves together and managed to win the game and the tournament. We talked and laughed about that night for years, most of us forgetting if we had won or lost, but we all remembered the fun and the bond that was created.

The leadership style that worked for me

My respect for LeRoy grew as I appreciated how he took the high road and just rolled with the punches. LeRoy's wisdom was in knowing that the actions of the team were no reflection on him, nor a measure of our respect or commitment to the team. He saw it for what it was—just a group of young guys acting stupid.

I cherished my first few years playing soccer, but it wouldn't last. The following year, the coaching position was vacant, and as the season was about to start, Ray Cardis was appointed as our new coach. Ray was an interesting guy, a rule follower and a traditional and conservative thinker. He was the trainer for the hockey team, had no coaching experience, and unfortunately for me, happened to be the Assistant Dean of Men's Residence, which meant he and I had had a few run-ins over the years.

One night, as I was returning to campus after an out-of-town soccer game, I asked the driver to stop the bus at my residence to save me the walk up the hill. It was no big deal; the driver had stopped there many times over the years, but Ray, eager to demonstrate his grandiose authority, refused to let the driver stop. Of course, this led me to tell Ray to "fuck right off!" The next day, he told me I'd have to apologize to him in front of everyone or I was off the team. Because that was never going to happen, I once again told him to "fuck off," and my soccer career was over. No regrets!

These experiences with LeRoy, Ray, and other self-proclaimed leaders were my first real experiences with leadership. It made me wonder: *What makes a person respect one coach and not another? What makes one team excel and another fail?* Mostly, it made me wonder what kind of leadership style would work for me.

I'm sure that Ray did what he thought was right. His actions were surely driven by his own experiences, biases, and the books on soccer and leadership he was always reading. In comparison, LeRoy also relied on his own experiences to guide his coaching philosophy, yet they were so different. Ray needed control, and LeRoy could just let it roll.

I knew from these experiences that I could never be committed to a team purely because I wore their jersey. I could never follow someone solely because they were called captain, coach, president, or leader. Most certainly, I would never be browbeaten into giving up 'me' to be part of 'we.'

Learning by doing (the wrong things)

Time rolled by, and during my third year, a couple of guys moved into Holy Cross from Niagara Falls, Ontario. John Vanderzanden and Tom Laslo were so damn cool. They never got too excited about anything and got along with everyone. It took a while for us to connect. They liked my girlfriend Jane and thought I came across as an idiot. They would ask people, "Why is she with that asshole?"

Still, we quickly got to know each other, and magic happened. Our connection was strong, causing us to spend countless hours skipping class, smoking dope, and playing backgammon, often interrupted by some kind of foolishness. Man, it was fun!

They always had my back. And yet, they never hesitated to tell me when I was being an ass. John V. once told me, "Rick, you have to take more crap from people because you give more."

I replied, "What? Okay, fair enough!"

Everyone gathered in the TV room in Holy Cross to watch our favorite shows. The room was filled with your run-of-the-mill, not-so-comfy wooden chairs. But this one guy had brought in his own big, comfy La-Zy-Boy chair from home. We couldn't be more jealous of his self-proclaimed throne.

It was a beat-up old thing, but compared to our hard splintered benches, it looked damn good to us. We had decided we hated the chair guy, so one night, when he wasn't around, John and I took his chair to the soccer practice field between Holy Cross and Vanier Hall, and we set it on fire.

We thought it would be a nice slow-burn, controlled blaze that we could dance around for a few minutes. It turned out to be quite the opposite. The moment we lit it, the La-Zy-Boy burst into flames that shot thirty feet into the air. We instantly knew we were in big trouble.

The lights went on in every room in both residences. The next thing we knew, the fire trucks arrived with the cops close behind, looking for the culprits. I could hear them standing outside my door, listening for any noise. I was breathing heavily, but I put a pillow over my head and managed to muffle the sound enough so they couldn't hear.

On another occasion, the three of us were downtown at a bar, and we and a few others got a ride back up the hill in the back of a pickup. It had a covered truck bed, and the owner had put in four-foot-long logs for added weight so he wouldn't slide on frosty winter nights.

I'm not sure whose idea it was, but someone started throwing the logs out of the back of the truck as we went up the hill. The logs would bounce down the middle of the street, causing the cars behind us to swerve around them as best they could. Soon, we saw a police car behind us with lights and sirens blazing, and still, someone kept tossing out the logs. To try to escape, the driver was taking quick turns through the streets, then people started jumping out of the back, and we followed suit, bouncing to our escape.

Kick away!

My girlfriend during most of my university years was Jane Forestell. She was beautiful, smart, and the star of the field hockey team; why she was with me was a mystery to everyone. I was up to no good most of the time—drunk, stoned, and on more than one occasion, not so nice to her. We would break up and get back together frequently, and during those breakup periods, I would, of course, act like the idiot I was! I'd stand outside her window at Vanier Hall like a shitty John Cusack without the boom box, yelling nasty remarks to get her attention. The lights would turn on throughout the residence, and the other girls would watch my performance.

As you can imagine, my messed-up little Romeo routine didn't exactly make me Mr. Popular with the Vanier ladies. So, I told John V., "If I end up under that damn window again, kick my ass back up the hill." Within a week, there I was, drunk and stoned, professing my love and hatred outside Jane's window. John, true to his word, started to kick me in the ass, over and over, as the girls watched from their windows above, yelling, "Kick him again; kick him harder!" And he did, all the way up the hill. I guess that's what friends are for, to give you a kick in the ass when you need it most.

Examining your regrets is worth the pain

The crazy thing was that this was a girl I loved deeply, but between the drinking and the demons that raged inside me, I was incapable of acting appropriately, of being a normal, decent guy.

Looking back, I could excuse my actions as drunken party mistakes, but in reality, it goes deeper than that. I wanted to be the big man on campus, to be identified as the wild party guy! Yet, undoubtedly, my actions boiled down to my overcompensating for my shortcomings, my insecurities that were eating me alive, and, well, just being a gaping dickhole.

The year after I finished university, Jane and I finally broke up for good. She came down with a serious medical issue and ended up having surgery while I was down in Florida, partying it up with my buddies. My mother decided not to tell me about Jane's medical emergency. When I finally got the news, I returned home, but by then, it was too little too late, and that pretty much did us in—that and the 1,000 other shitty things I had done.

I went back to Saint Thomas a few times to go to pubs or play in sporting events. Sometimes I saw her, we talked, and our connection was always strong. But she eventually moved on and started dating the quarterback of the UNB football team while I continued down my path to nowhere. I've thought a lot about Jane over the years, deeply regretting my actions, and wishing I could have been a better person. But that was me at the time; I didn't show respect to anyone outside my circle of friends, not even my girlfriend. I was on a one-way mission, with a total focus on me.

I learned through these years that your perspective of what a leader should look like is fundamental to how each of us acts as a leader. Ray's perspective of what a leader could do and his resulting approach brought out the worst in me, while LeRoy's guidance, flexibility, and let-it-roll attitude brought out the best.

I also came to understand that the makeup of a team was fundamental to the cohesion and the resulting performance of that team. My experiences with the hockey and soccer teams were very different. Even though both teams had many of the same players, the addition of a few disruptive forces changed the dynamic of each team and, ultimately, its performance. It would be these lessons from hockey and soccer, Ray and LeRoy, and the swim team that would further embed in me a certain leadership code.

It was still early in my life's journey, and I still had a lot to learn and personal issues to figure out. My inappropriate actions gave me a long list of regrets that would gnaw away at me and, over time, instilled in me the need to be a better person.

As crazy as it sounds, the cheating I did in school was essential to my development. I was learning how to survive in a world built for others, finding ways to jump the hurdles put in front of me, be creative, and not let society's rules define what I could or could not be.

Of course, I wouldn't suggest cheating to anyone else, yet we all have to find our path, come to terms with who we are, understand our skills, and then cling to them unapologetically.

As my final year drew to a close, I had no plan, so I headed back to the Miramichi, took my job as a lifeguard for the summer, and decided to figure it out from there.

Key takeaways

- Your perception of what a leader should be will have everything to do with the leader you'll become. Make sure you get it right.
- Use your regrets to fuel positive change.

LESSON 5

Listen, learn, and adapt, but never lose yourself in the process

I am always ready to learn, although I do not always like being taught.

Winston Churchill

The next chapter of my life taught me a lot about humility and the need to embrace change. Failing and doing the same thing all over again is the definition of madness. I needed to fail. I needed to understand where I needed help, and what I wasn't so good at. Later on, as I was put in management positions, I used this practical knowledge and sense of myself to surround myself with people who had the skills that I lacked and the ability to keep me in check.

When my time at Saint Thomas was over, I went out into the real world. My first bonehead move was at the week-long National Lifeguard Certificate program, where the instructors thought I had a 'piss-poor' attitude. When I thought I was being cool, they saw me as arrogant. To them, I looked out of shape, but in my eyes, I was an elite swimmer. When I stayed out at bars every night, they thought I wasn't taking the program seriously, while I saw myself as independent and, well, nobody could tell *me* what to do!

As a result of my poor attitude and delusional thinking, they failed my ass. This failure was a monumental blow to my ego. Swimming was my thing, maybe my only thing. Many of the kids I had trained who had half my ability passed the course easily. The whole situation was so embarrassing and made it painfully obvious that my approach to people and life was not going to cut it. Something had to change, but I didn't have a clue where to even start.

The Miramichi was an interesting place to live, with loads of friendly and wonderful people. I adhered to my party-hard scheme for a while, but even with all this excitement, time was getting long on the Miramichi. Based on my coaching success (the only thing I seemed to be good at), I applied and was accepted into the Graduate Diploma in Sports Administration (DSA) program at Concordia University in Montreal. So, off I went, back to a city I loved.

Myth: You have to be intelligent to succeed

Everywhere I went, I always managed to find the top partiers, and Concordia would be no exception. The first guy I met was Bill Haggerty. Bill had no boundaries and was a Hollywood-caliber partier. I'll never forget him running naked through the residence, chasing some girlfriend of his, and then walking slowly back to his room without a care in the world or a stitch of clothing. Bill had a network of friends from his years at Stanstead College, a private boarding school in the Eastern Townships of Quebec, many of whom went to Concordia.

After a few weeks of heavy partying with Bill and the boys, school began, and once again, it became clear that all this academic stuff was way over my head. Finance, statistics, and accounting were like Egyptian hieroglyphics. I couldn't make hide nor hair of any of the material.

I soon came to the realization that, once again, I'd have to work outside the lines if I hoped to succeed.

As part of the DSA program, everyone had to do an internship, which I started at the Olympic pool and would later complete at Sport Nova Scotia in Halifax. I learned from working in these nonprofit and volunteer organizations that their mandate and operating style didn't match up with my needs. There just wasn't enough structure or accountability. They lacked the clear and defined direction that I intuitively knew I must have if I had any hope of getting anything accomplished.

Wait, I'm not immortal?

I made a lot of good friends at Concordia. One of them was Bill Brant, who owned a bar and hotel in Magog, Quebec. He and I had a bet once: If I did something (I can't remember what), he'd let me and the boys drink for free at his bar. It was game on, I won the bet, and a date was set. That weekend was a total Gong Show, and our all-expenses-paid party night was totally out of control. But he couldn't very well kick us out when we were his special VIP guests. He might not have thought that through!

Bill Brant died a few years later. There was an accident at the local marina, and he was found floating in the bay. Bill was classy, smart, good-looking, personable, beastly strong, and as fit as any man could be. I considered him downright invincible. Hearing that he died made me think hard about life and how lucky my friends and I were to have survived the craziness and that maybe none of us were that invincible after all.

The year at Concordia was a good one. I had a blast, made some great friends, and even managed to creatively claw my way through and pass. But I still had no job or prospects. With no clear path forward, I once again retreated to the Miramichi.

Me and my cracked foundation

I think it's safe to say that nobody, including myself, believed I was on the road to having a successful career or becoming a strong leader. The sad reality was that most people saw me as this disrespectful, insensitive, selfish, and inappropriate guy, willing to cheat and break the rules whenever it suited my purpose and with quite a knack for alienating people. To top it off, I had few of the skills that might allow me to beat the odds and make a comeback: I had a seemingly below-average IQ and writing skills that would embarrass an eight-year-old, and I was dealing with some sort of learning disability.

I was always told that it's your early years that lay the foundation for the person you'll become and that establish the core values that will determine your future actions. Well, I'd have been the first to admit that my foundation looked pretty cracked and compromised. So, how the hell did I get from this version of myself to the person that people would someday call a leader?

Searching for answers, I started to look deeper, past my obvious indiscretions and countless flaws, for what might be hiding beneath the surface. I knew my brain was wired differently, causing me to see people, actions, and events through a very different lens than most.

I came to understand that my life experiences instilled in me my own set of biases, values, and beliefs. Having been bullied caused me to often push back and always question authority. Doing poorly in school forced me to get out of the box and find creative ways to succeed. My regrets caused me to often reexamine my actions and search for a better way to get things done. Being a perpetual rule breaker allowed me to be comfortable not always pleasing the person in charge, while the support and acceptance of my friends gave me the sense that I was okay.

From my experience with the swim team, soccer, and hockey, Ray, and LeRoy, I learned that leading a group of people had everything to do with enthusiasm, commitment, and connection. I came to understand that leadership wasn't so much about demand and control as it was about respect and trust. I realized that the secret to team success was creating an environment where hard work and fun felt like the same thing.

Eureka moment for the atypical underdogs out there

One day, I had this crazy thought. Could the very things that I thought were holding me back—my faults, disabilities, and limitations—have given me a perspective, skill set, and leadership advantage over the intelligent, talented high achievers who rarely experienced defeat, ridicule, or regret?

Many years later, I found validation for my wild idea in a book titled *The Disabled Leader*.[2] "Understand your capabilities and limitations… Just because you perceive yourself to have a limitation does not mean that you lack the ability to develop skills." The author goes on to explain how physically disabled leaders often demonstrate leadership traits better than the general population.

When you are an 'atypical' living in a world designed for a standardized way of thinking and everything you do seems counterintuitive, wrong, or inappropriate, this forces you to reconsider your actions, reevaluate your approach, and look for alternate ways to get things done. The end product of this process is none other than self-awareness. A powerful tool.

Key takeaways

- Blunders are just moments in time; let them go.
- Let your unique perspective power your actions.

LESSON 6

Smart people accept help

I cannot give you the formula for success, but I can give you the formula for failure, which is: Try to please everybody.

Herbert Swope

It is not easy to make something of yourself when the world expects little of you. This is both the curse and the blessing of 'atypicals.' There is a kind of freedom in knowing nobody is watching your every move or has designs on what you should become. The freedom to push boundaries and embrace your uniqueness allows you to become comfortable with who you really are.

My journey would have been very different if I had not accepted the opportunity that was presented to me as I frolicked aimlessly around the Miramichi. The challenges ahead would push me to look inside myself, dramatically increasing my awareness of how important it was to learn, adapt, and surround myself with the right kind of people.

I was unemployed, with no prospects of a job, and out of the blue, my brother Carl called me to tell me that his buddy, Norm Teske, who worked in the corporate offices of Pharmaprix (Shoppers Drug Mart in Quebec), had convinced the manager at the flagship store in Montreal to bring me on as a manager trainee.

Not in my wildest dreams had I ever imagined working for a pharmacy (I'm not sure I even knew what a pharmacy was), but because I didn't have a lot of options, I jumped at the opportunity. I was also eager to reconnect with my friends from Concordia.

As a management trainee, I did every job: sweeping floors, taking out the garbage, cashier, stocking the shelves, anything and everything.

I was under the watchful eye of Guy Melancon, the experienced and highly respected store manager. So, I'd be able to learn from one of the best in the business.

Because the store was directly below the Pharmaprix corporate offices, I got to know several executives and even played hockey with them once a week. When I was a kid, my mother always talked about the 'big shots' in town and gave me the impression that they had some kind of special ability, a certain kind of magic that I could never have. Yet, as I listened to these guys talk about business and their personal lives, they seemed no different from me.

Who the hell do you think you are?

As I got promoted and took on new responsibilities, I was asked by Guy to make sure that the executives from upstairs didn't make merchandising changes in the store without asking him or the store owner, Arnie Smith. Being the faithful soldier I was, I planned to uphold their command.

One day, the VP of Marketing was discussing store shelf changes with a vendor, and I intervened. "I'd have to talk to Guy to see if that would be possible," I piped in. Oh, boy. You'd swear I stole his lunch money. He immediately ushered me to his office, where he masterfully ripped a piece off me "How dare you question my actions!" he said. "Who the hell do you think you are?" He also uttered a few other choice remarks.

I was perplexed. I did what I was asked to do but ended up getting in big trouble. The funny thing was that I had a great relationship with the VP of Marketing, but when he thought I was challenging his authority, he turned on me in an instant. Lesson learned!

Working under Guy was an exceptional experience. He was professional, focused, organized, and relaxed at the same time. He let me run with the ball, believed in me, and trusted me. In time, it would be his belief in me that would give me a newfound sense of confidence.

Starting to want more

Outside of work, I was still the same old me, focused on having fun and happy to hang with my friends. To get around town, I bought a car, a very second-hand Datsun 240Z. It was a rusty old piece of crap, but I loved it. I had a guy do some bodywork and did what I could myself. I had the mechanical know-how of a sorority sister, but when you can see the pavement under your feet, you do what you need to do.

To paint a more vivid image of my 'vintage' ride, picture this: When I drove to work in the rain, I'd be gripping a rope with my right hand to hold the passenger door closed. Simultaneously, with my left hand, I'd carefully puppeteer the various strings that operated the windshield wipers. I'd steer with my knees and keep fantastic posture because the driver seat would routinely fall flat if the vehicle halted. Multitasking at its best!

My eighteen months at Pharmaprix went by quickly. Working every job gave me a solid foundation, and it would be this deep understanding of the pieces of the business that would prove irreplaceable as I moved forward in my career.

With my training complete, it was time to move on and find a store of my own. Because I didn't speak French (which seemed impossible for me), I knew that a career with Pharmaprix was pretty much impossible, so I started looking for opportunities beyond Quebec.

My brother's pal Norm came to my aid once more and contacted Ed Parker at the SDM Atlantic office, and as luck would have it, the Douglastown Shoppers Drug Mart directly across the river from my parents' house was looking for a manager. I had a talk with the owner, David Skidd, and with a little help from relatives of mine who knew David, I got the job. So, I packed my bags and hit the road.

Understanding what's important

David, my new boss, was a real gentleman and the most laid-back guy I've ever met. He gave me free rein to manage the front of the store. It was a huge opportunity, and I knew I couldn't afford to screw it up.

To bridge the gap of my inexperience, I tapped into the knowledge and candor of the manager down the street. Joanne LeBlanc was a ball of fire. Loud and outspoken, she talked like a longshoreman, was funny as hell, and could party like a rock star. In her, I met my match. She took none of my crap, forcing me to do things her way, usually the right way. Joanne wasn't smooth or polished—quite the opposite—but she had integrity, and it was that one quality that caused so many people to respect and trust her. I only had eighteen months of retail experience when I first started dealing with Joanne, and I used to ask her the stupidest questions, to which she'd reply, "Jesus Christ, don't you know anything?" And then we'd laugh.

Despite her brash ways, husky voice, and foul language, Joanne could make her staff feel at ease and empowered, a skill I knew I still had to develop.

I went ahead and took a course through SDM's Learning Academy that focused on the book, *The One Minute Manager*, a literary sensation at the time.

For some reason, the book struck a chord in me. It put things simply and straightforwardly that I, of all people, could understand. I must have read it twenty times as I worked at implementing its simple principles. And, lo and behold, I started to see a difference in my employees. Their body language changed, they seemed more relaxed, our conversations became more meaningful, and everyone just seemed happier. Then the store started to hum like a fine sports car, and our productivity improved to become the highest in Atlantic Canada.

The turnaround was remarkable. I couldn't help but think back to my years with the swim team and how finding the right balance between hard work and a positive environment invariably led to superior performance.

Finding the right fit

In my personal life, I was dating my future wife, Monique, and traveling to Fredericton on most weekends. That prompted me to apply for the manager's job at the Regent Street store in Fredericton, but the owner and I didn't connect. I think I came across as bold and brash for him, and the job went to someone else.

I remember being so disappointed, and then, as luck would have it, a few days later, the regional office called me and offered me a job as a district manager. They were looking for a young university graduate with some experience operating a store, and they actually *wanted* someone who was bold and brash, capable of handling store owners.

It was an unbelievable turn of events. The disappointment and embarrassment of not getting one job morphed into the opportunity of a lifetime

In June 1984, I started working at SDM Atlantic's regional office. It wouldn't take long for me to realize that working at the head office was a very different world. I quickly understood that I'd have to adapt fast or get run over. By sheer coincidence, my good friend John MacIntyre joined the regional office on the same day as me in the role of Marketing Manager.

Finding that special friend

Johnny Mac had been the manager of the Port Hawkesbury (Nova Scotia) stores, and we had struck up a friendship at a management training course in Cape Breton. The first night, an excellent band was playing at the hotel bar. Neither of us could resist the bait, and we commenced the bonding. We were drawn to each other like two hard rock fans at a Barry Manilow concert. The night was completely off the rails, and the friendship was sealed.

The next morning, we had deadly hangovers, but we knew we couldn't miss the morning session. We sat beside each other, and just before the break, things took a turn. I could feel my tongue start to swell, and I could tell an explosion was imminent. I said to Johnny, "I don't feel good." I shot out of my seat and out of the room.

As soon as I shut the door behind me, puke exploded from my mouth, shooting across the hallway. I put my hand over my mouth, but all that did was expand the blast radius of the vomit, which shot through my fingers in all directions. I continued emptying the contents of my stomach on the carpet just outside the conference room. When the vomiting paused for a moment, I ran off to the washroom and cleaned up, but as I headed back in, I realized that last night's Jack Daniels and three a.m. pizza were still painted on the carpet outside the meeting room.

This meeting room contained the executives who would determine my future. If I didn't get the contents of my stomach cleaned up, my career at Shoppers Drug Mart might be a very short one.

I found a paper towel and franticly wiped up the vomit, holding my breath and trying not to puke again in response to the wretched smell. I swear, the second I was done, the doors to the meeting room flew open, and the group filed out onto the newly-cleaned carpet. Luckily for me, no one had any idea of what had happened. Well, except Johnny, and he wouldn't tell, as would be the case with so many secrets we would share in the years to come.

That day marked the beginning of a friendship and working partnership that would span forty years. Johnny Mac, his wife Bev, Monique, and I would share countless adventures together. I am a different guy today as a result of my relationship with Johnny Mac. He was smart, he had class, and there was no way a bit of it wouldn't rub off on me.

Watching Johnny in action elevated me to a high standard of professionalism that I could have never achieved on my own.

Turning my foe into my greatest ally

Another guy I had a strong connection with during those years was Dan White, who would turn out to be a key player throughout my career. When Dan first came to SDM, he and I didn't see eye to eye. The staff at my stores were complaining that the warehouse was underperforming; inventories were low, service was poor, and deliveries were late. To see if we could resolve our differences, Dan suggested that we take a trip, visit a few of the stores, have a drink, and maybe get to know each other better.

I must confess that when we set off on the trip, my attitude was, "I'll show him!" As we visited various stores and listened to their issues, Dan pulled out various reports and delivery schedules, and it quickly became apparent that the store managers and employees were causing their own problems. *Damn, he was right*, I thought. *The bastard!*

Dan taught me a monumental lesson during those few days together: Just because people say things are one way or the other, it doesn't make it so.

This piece of wisdom would become entrenched in my thinking. From that day forward, I'd always be sure to get the facts (the real facts), try to understand the issue and the people involved, and then come to a decision.

No one gets a free pass

This creed encapsulated how we operated as a group; no one got a free pass. Being buddies didn't mean anything. No one rolled over or compromised on important issues—hell no!

Over the years, I have seen so much manipulation of information, deception, baseless rumors, and smooth talkers convincing others to swallow their crap. I was determined to come to my own opinion on people and events, no matter how compelling the stories, no matter how solid the facts might seem at first glance.

Putting on my 'big boy' pants

I worked under many bosses during the early days of my career, and there were some interesting ones. One of them was Lennie Burke, a down-to-earth good old boy who took me under his wing, pointed me in the right direction, and helped me navigate the complexities that came from working in the office.

We developed a strong relationship, leading to countless nights in the company of Lennie and his girlfriend Duckie. As the years went by and I gained more responsibility, I had to make some tough decisions, and we eventually drifted apart. Essentially, he thought I should have had his back more, and maybe he was right. We both left the company in 2000, and I never saw Lennie again. He died a few years ago, and I always felt guilty for not having made the trip to his home in Bathurst (New Brunswick) to talk things out, a regret I will carry with me forever.

My error in dealing with Lennie had little to do with the decisions I made—they were no- brainers—but I should have had the gumption to sit down with him and talk things through. He would have been pissed, and the conversation would have been uncomfortable for me, but it would have been the right thing to do.

This experience taught me that regardless of how difficult any conversation might be, I needed to put on my 'big boy' pants and deal with issues head-on.

Throughout this period in my life, the help I received from people like Norm, Guy, David, Joanne, Johnny, Dan, and Lennie was truly a gift. Watching them give away their knowledge and wisdom for free, without the expectation of getting anything in return, instilled in me a desire to do the same for others as I moved forward in my career.

I learned from them that asking for help, giving help, and accepting help are essential to teamwork and leadership.

But the lesson goes much deeper. What they gave to me, well in advance of our developing close relationships, was pretty astonishing. Their gift was immediate, with no political agenda and no need for reciprocal action. Just a no-strings-attached sharing of their knowledge and know-how.

They were demonstrating a quality I didn't have or understand at the time, and it would be their influence that would cause me to abandon my selfish and self-serving mindset, developing in me a want, almost a need, to live up to their standards.

As you grow in your career and move closer to leadership, you'll need to share your knowledge and inspire others, not for recognition or rewards but simply because it's the right thing to do.

This all may sound mighty wise, but in fact, I was in the earliest stages of my learning curve. There was so much I didn't know, with many more bridges to cross and, undoubtedly, a few to burn.

Key takeaways

- Build strong, meaningful relationships with people who both support and challenge you.
- The strength of someone's belief is not a measure of the truth.
- Asking for help is a display of confidence.

LESSON 7

Half of leadership is just being organized

All men have fears, but the brave put down their fears and go forward.

Dale Carnegie

In my first role as a district manager, I was sent out on the road with virtually no formal direction, just a mandate to 'make things happen,' whatever that meant. The owners, in those days, ran their stores as they saw fit. They were fearlessly independent and had little trust or respect for the head office.

Whenever I made a comment or recommendation, they immediately took it to be baseless criticism of their business, or worse, personal attacks on themselves.

In an attempt to breach their skepticism, I started asking, "What do you expect of me?" And, "How can I help you?" Almost immediately, their tone changed. As I gave away control of the agenda, they seemed to lower their guard, allowing us to get down to business.

I soon understood that this leadership role I was placed in wasn't so much about demand and control but discussion and support. As soon as the store owners' guard was down, I tried to steer the conversation toward improving the business, aka putting more money in their pockets.

I soon realized, however, that many of the stores struggled to successfully complete even the simplest of tasks. They operated in a world where everyone was responsible for everything, which in my mind meant that no one was responsible for anything. I turned my attention to getting the staff organized, looking at who did what, when, where, and for how long.

The simplest things mean so much!

Store management and I started by realigning employee duties, ensuring people had the time required to do their job, eliminating interruptions, balancing workloads, establishing accountabilities, creating job descriptions, and developing individual work plans. As we implemented this new approach, we initially encountered lots of skepticism, but it wouldn't be long before the staff was praising the new system.

In the end, the results of the new way of doing things were astonishing: employee satisfaction and productivity soared, the stores' image improved, service levels increased, customer feedback was incredibly positive, and, most importantly, there was growth in every single store's bottom line.

It became crystal-clear to me that organization, clarity, and accountability were at the core of outstanding performance.

Due to the success of my territory, I was moved to other underperforming territories, finally landing in Halifax, soon to be under attack by Walmart.

The owners were shaking in their boots with the prospect of Walmart coming to Canada and expected both stores' sales and profitability to be decimated.

When good is just not good enough

When I arrived in Halifax, we'd evaluated our preparedness and agreed that things had to change fast—or Walmart was going to eat us for lunch.

I challenged the store owners to start acting like one collective team, which I knew would be a monumental change for these people who took great satisfaction in being the kings of their castles.

I knew we'd have to raise the bar on our performance and expect more from ourselves and our employees. It was clear that what had once been good was no longer good enough.

We set a new operational standard, created a management action committee, developed a strategic plan, created a new local marketing and advertising program, updated our pricing policy, improved store image, and increased service levels.

We knew that if we were going to keep our customers, we needed to create a more customer-centric environment, and the first step to doing that was ensuring we had a happy and motivated workforce. We did the usual stuff: staff meetings to keep them informed, staff surveys to listen to their concerns, and a revision of our wage and benefits policies to be more competitive, yet none of this was where the real magic was to be found.

Finding our groove

Aside from all these improvements, if we wanted to truly energize the team, we'd have to think outside the box. We decided to organize a series of social events where staff and management could mingle and have a little fun. Skit Night was born.

We rented a hall where each store, as well as the office, would put on skits. I have personally performed the moonwalk to Michael Jackson's "Beat It," played Hanz in "I'll pump you up" from *Saturday Night Live*, and displayed my lack of talent in other embarrassing displays.

It was a huge success. The fact that the office and store managers were getting involved in this type of activity showed employees that we could have fun, laugh at ourselves, and just be part of the crowd.

The fun we had and the friendships we built carried over into the workweek and drastically changed the relationship between the staff, management, and the office. Everyone felt like they belonged; we all became one team with one mission. None of what we did was company-prescribed, created in a boardroom, or handed down to us from above. We stepped out of the box, accepted our challenges and the associated risks, and then pushed forward with a total commitment to getting things done.

This change in the dynamic created a sense of ownership that caused our employees to truly care about their store's success and hence our customers. Customers, in turn, could feel the positive vibe, resulting in a radical improvement in customer satisfaction and retention.

We later added other activities, such as floor hockey, ice hockey, softball, and curling tournaments, as well as bar-hopping events. Each of these community-building activities helped to keep the special atmosphere alive, leading to some pretty remarkable results.

Through this period, while the rest of the region was in free fall, this group of stores that represented twenty percent of the sales volume in Atlantic Canada went on to produce sixty-five percent of the profitability, while productivity and other operational metrics soared.

Don't get me wrong; it wasn't always fun and games. Hard work and performance mattered; sales, profitability, and strong KPIs (key performance indicators) were all part of the winning formula. On occasion, people failed to live up to their end of the bargain, and, unfortunately for them, there were consequences.

With all this talk of fun, connection, trust, and respect, you need to understand that there are fundamental requirements to getting your objectives accomplished. Good intentions and a happy team by themselves won't get you there.

Key takeaways

- Keep leadership in perspective. It's not the movies; it's just creating the right conditions for people to succeed.
- A high-functioning team is greater than the sum of its parts.

LESSON 8

Be bold and prepared to take crap for doing the right thing

Do the right thing. It will gratify some people and astonish the rest.

Mark Twain

As I established myself as a manager capable of producing outstanding results, I had to make some tough decisions, which led to people blaming me for their demise, almost as if I had stabbed them in the back. This type of criticism caused me to reexamine my actions that led to employee dismissals. Was I the monster they told everyone I was, or were they just looking for someone to blame besides themselves?

After some reflection and a lot of soul-searching, I figured my decisions were the right ones, but my actions needed a little tweaking. Sure, I had checked all the boxes before making the decision to fire someone. Before it came to that, however, I may have cowered when it came time to have the tough, no-holds-barred conversation about each person's performance and the potential consequences of underperforming.

This caused me to readjust my approach, and I made a personal oath to myself to always say what needed to be said and never hold back, regardless of how uncomfortable the conversation might be for either party.

My new, unwavering commitment to straightforwardness would raise a few eyebrows along the way and became a trademark of my management style.

It always flows downhill

On some occasions, and with the approval of regional management, I had to terminate store owners. As you can imagine, folks with the title of 'owner' don't take this sort of news in stride, particularly when it's coming from a young, hotshot regional manager.

That was the case with the owner of our downtown Halifax location, whom I had been approved to let go. He was not very pleased with the decision and quite literally swore his revenge.

A few months later, I was sitting at home when I received a phone call from Herb Binder, the president of Shoppers Drug Mart. Now, you need to appreciate that I was just the district manager in Halifax at the time; I was not sure he even knew I existed.

He said, "Rick, it's Herb Binder." I was blown away that he was calling me, and he could hear that in my voice. He said, "I am calling you about the letter you sent me regarding Harry's horrible performance." I was shocked; Harry was my boss. As I tried to pick my jaw up off the floor, I asked, "Um, what letter?" I truly had no idea what he was talking about! He explained that he had received a letter signed by me, Rick Brennan, describing Harry's shortcomings in minute detail.

Thankfully, Herb believed me, and as far as he was concerned, that was that. I cannot say the same about Harry, who was infuriated and, as

I would soon find out, looking for his own 'pound of flesh.' Whoever wrote the letter was smart. They didn't go after me; they made it look like I was attacking my superior and then sent it to the president of the company. Genius! Not too long after that at a buying show in Toronto, Harry booked a meeting with me. He didn't summon me to praise my performance. On the contrary, he went up one side of me and down the other, making up outrageous claims as he did his little war dance.

I was never made aware of the full content of the letter, but I guess some of it was accurate. Harry probably knew there was some truth in my supposed criticism of him and assumed I agreed with it, which I probably did. Interestingly enough, my instinct after watching Harry's little war dance was not to be more cautious and politically correct. Hell no! It was defiance. There was no way I would allow his shortcomings to impact my operating style, which would only serve to nullify my effectiveness. I have often thought it was too bad that Harry couldn't just laugh about the letter and show just a touch of humility. What a difference it would have made to me and everyone involved.

If everyone loves you, you can't be doing much

I have no proof that the disgruntled store owner was the author of that fateful letter. But the whole experience taught me that I was okay with dealing with the negative consequences of doing what I thought was right. It was not in my nature to be diplomatic and political or to tell lies and give unwarranted compliments to advance my career.

Early in my management training, I learned that I had to be strategic with authority figures if I wanted to keep my job. But I am proud to say that I never allowed Harry or any other boss to browbeat me into being someone I was not.

It was never easy. It takes a certain strength to weather these kinds of storms, but I think there is no way to successfully lead a team without it.

Making mistakes is inevitable, and learning from them is essential. You need to be bold, creative, assertive, and comfortable taking risks; it's key to leading a team. Unfortunately, you can't always predict the outcome of even the best-laid plans. My actions to have the owner in Halifax removed had been approved by Harry, and each of his directives was followed to the T. Harry's reaction to the admittedly odd circumstances was fueled by his egoistical instincts, which I could not control. Other bosses (past and future) would have just ignored the letter, praised my efforts, and moved on.

Let's face it, what constitutes a mistake or good or bad performance is based on opinion, personality, circumstances, timing, and agenda. So, don't try to predict the future; just do what you think is right with the information at hand, and let the cards fall where they may.

The other option is to do nothing, and that is not an option for us 'atypicals.'

Key takeaways
- Accepting risk is an unavoidable consequence of leadership if you hope to get anything accomplished.
- All you can ever do is make decisions with the information at hand, and then let the chips fall where they may.

LESSON 9

Take the time to understand your limitations

Our only limitations are those we set up in our minds.

Napoleon Hill

Despite the letter and Harry's bellicose attitude, my store's performance numbers excelled during this period. I was at the top of my game. I was well-respected by the owners and managers of my stores and my peers. Most likely saw me as a sort of intelligent guy, but in reality, it was all a sham. I had done a good job hiding my limitations and disguising my disabilities, relying on my executive assistants to handle my written correspondence and mastering a short and simple form of mental math that allowed me to approximate numbers pretty accurately.

Regardless of my success, I often felt confused, stupid, and incapable of executing the simplest tasks. Besides, I had become a parent by then, and I needed to better understand my issues just in case my children might face the same types of challenges. That's why I decided to get tested by a psychologist to see if we could figure out what the hell was wrong with me.

I underwent a series of tests, which determined that I had serious cognitive processing issues. My ability to process and retain information was measured at seventeen percent. There were also signs of dyslexia, dyscalculia, and a few other conditions. I always knew I had some sort of problem, so the results weren't a total surprise, but what blew me away was that the tests also showed that my comprehension was at ninety-five percent, a very high score.

The psychologist explained that over the years, I had developed coping skills that allowed me to see the big picture despite not understanding the details. She told me I had somehow learned to see past the clutter and mounds of information, quickly recognizing the underlying core issues and identifying potential solutions.

This new understanding of how my brain worked was truly a life-altering moment. I felt I was getting closer to every philosopher's dream, the elusive chimera of knowing oneself. I finally understood why I excelled at certain things and sucked at others; why I needed to write things down on paper, be organized, keep things simple, work off lists, and leave nothing to memory.

As my psychologist put it, I needed to declutter my brain's plate. When I wrote things down on a list, that simple act opened up space in my working brain, leaving more room for me to process other information. That explained why I could do something on Monday but was unable to do the same thing on a busy Tuesday. It all made sense.

After this revelatory psychological assessment, I knew to trust my perspective rather than constantly second-guessing myself. Until that moment, there was always a feeling in the back of my mind that I might be totally wrong—that my brain was perhaps not firing on all cylinders. Understanding how my brain operated and the successful coping strategies I had developed over the years imbued me with a newfound self-confidence. In understanding my limitations, I found freedom.

My newly acquired self-awareness also helped me deal with my anxiety, which often had me in its grip. At times, I just couldn't stop that revved-up feeling; it was like I had a fringing chemical imbalance. After the psychological assessment, I had the comfort of knowing that my brain was just wired differently, which helped me to relax and slow down my thoughts, and that gradually reduced that annoying revved-up feeling.

Searching for more answers

Reading books like Eckart Tolle's *The Power of Now*[3] helped me develop a more positive perspective on life, teaching me to better enjoy the moment rather than dwelling on the regrets of yesterday or what tomorrow may or may not bring. Sitting down and smoking a joint also helped take the edge off; it was like a whole other side of my brain opened up. I became creative, relaxed, and funny. Interestingly, whenever I got on my wife's nerves, she often said, "Would you just go smoke a joint? I like you better that way." I knew to trust her advice and often obliged, and the powers of cannabis would help reset my brain from negative thoughts to a more positive outlook.

To try to help reduce my anxiety around public speaking, I took the Dale Carnegie training. Carnegie is the world-famous author of *How to Win Friends and Influence People*.[4] One of the strategies he proposes to get you out of your comfort zone is to have you talk about your life experiences to reveal your hardships and your most vulnerable moments. The stories I heard during those weekly Dale Carnegie sessions were powerful. I was so humbled and so impressed by people's resilience; it was inspiring. Listening to those stories made me realize that people are not always what they seem. That person you think is stuck-up is only shy; that person who's unresponsive is only trying to cope with their shit; those aggressive types, who on the surface seem so confident, are only trying to hide their anxiety and low self-esteem.

This new insight allowed me to see people through a different lens. I learned to see past their outward personas and realized there was always more to everyone's stories. I took the Dale Carnegie training several times, even becoming a teaching assistant (TA), a role that allowed me to expand my boundaries even further.

I know that public speaking is difficult for a lot of people, yet through the Dale Carnegie sessions, I came to understand that it's just another skill, like riding a bike or throwing a curveball. If you put the effort in, you can probably learn how to do it. Naturally, some will be better than others. Not everyone will develop a curveball that will take them to the major leagues, but we can still play the game.

I have always found it so ridiculous that people make a direct connection between great public speaking and leadership as if leadership was somehow defined by how convincing someone sounds behind a podium. In my experience, that is rarely the case. I have come across many a stellar speaker who couldn't lead a herd of sheep through an open gate into a pasture.

Deprogramming myself

Harry, my boss for years at Shoppers, became my teacher and mentor, and I learned a lot from him. But, as you may have already suspected from the story about the letter, he had a rough and self-serving management style. Over the years, Harry wrote my performance reviews, establishing what was right, wrong, acceptable, or unacceptable. If I wanted to get a good performance rating or get promoted, I had to do things his way and measure up to his standards.

Despite all my stubbornness, my commitment to doing things my way, and my belief that his approach sucked, Harry's influence was undeniable and, frankly, unavoidable. Many pieces of it stuck to me like glue.

As I moved on to other positions, experiencing other management styles and managing new teams, I began to understand the impact Harry had had on me. Over time, I had to consciously work on deprogramming myself so that I wouldn't do or say things that I had learned from Harry.

As I underwent this laborious transformation, I began to wonder why Harry dealt with people and events the way he did. I came to realize that he lacked one essential quality of leadership: humility. Harry's ego, his previous successes, and his high level of self-reliance made him believe that he had all the answers, which inevitably robbed him of the knowledge of what a highly motivated team could do for him.

Self-examination

I learned a lot during my Shoppers years, but the greatest gifts I received were the friendships of several wonderful people, the experiences we shared, and the fun we had, especially when we went a little overboard. Make no mistake; we worked hard. We were laser-focused on our goals, yet the fuel that drove our success was our culture of fun and our sense of belonging. We just couldn't get enough!

Identifying my own limitations was key in helping me understand other people's challenges and limitations. It also helped me relax and accept who I was, which included not having the same skills as others. I was different, but my brain had developed these alternative pathways to deal with my differences in my own unique way.

Then again, listening to people discuss their hardships and fears at Dale Carnegie sessions showed me that I was not the only one dealing with dysfunction and trauma. I learned that the self-confidence that comes from self-knowledge is much deeper and more sustainable.

Somehow, I stopped measuring myself with the same parameters. There was a different scale to measure someone like me, and I was excelling at it.

I owe many of these insights to the existence of my children. They made me think deeper about the workings of my issues and my position in the world. If it hadn't been for them, I probably wouldn't have undergone the psychological tests.

Getting to know myself better confirmed once more that knowledge was bliss, no matter how hard the truth. And truly understanding my limitations made all the difference.

Take inventory of your skills, and talk to a cross-section of people to validate that what you perceive as your strengths actually are your strengths. Then seek out the answers to what you don't understand; read books, attend seminars, and find ways to master your skills. You never know when you might uncover new insights.

Key takeaways

- Master and fully commit to your strengths.
- Only look to neutralize your weaknesses.
- You cannot be everything to everybody; stop trying.

LESSON 10

Mix business and personal as often as you can!

The rule of my life is to make business a pleasure, and pleasure my business.

Aaron Burr

I spent eighteen years at Shoppers Drug Mart, dividing my time between Halifax and Moncton. It was a time of working hard and reaching targets, but our main focus was all about having fun. Our expense accounts seemed limitless, and they were rarely scrutinized by the boss. We partied at every opportunity, and I was often the leader of the pack.

In those days, the regional executives perpetuated this party culture, organizing countless all-you-can-drink events where everyone was given the green light to let loose, and we were more than willing to oblige. These fun events became my connection point, allowing me to form relationships with people who would have a transformative impact on my life.

I had my own way of contributing to our 'culture.' I became famous for hitting the bars, partying my ass off, and then leaving my company credit card behind. I did it literally hundreds of times. It was so expected of me that after I left, the last person in our crowd knew to go to the bar and ask for Rick's card.

Among the events were the annual summer party and horseshoe tournament, where John and I always wore ridiculous costumes; the annual SDM golf tournament, where Dan and the rest of the team wore silly matching outfits; and the Digby Celebrity Golf Tournament, where there were essentially no rules at all. It was an endless agenda of craziness designed to show vendors and customers a good time and a wonderful excuse to expense mountains of booze.

The main corporate event of the year was the annual buying show in Toronto; it was our Super Bowl. My stores' management group and office friends would coordinate our activities before leaving, arranging to meet at a designated bar in the city, and the party would go into full swing, lasting until the wee hours of each day we were there.

I always got extremely hungover after a big night, which made getting to the meeting the next morning almost impossible. I often used a trick to get a little more recovery time. I rolled out of bed, got dressed, went downstairs, walked through the breakfast area (making sure I was seen by the bosses), and then headed straight back to my room to sleep until noon. With one thousand people at the meeting, no one was ever the wiser.

A round of rum-a-dumb

During these trips, Johnny, Dan, Lennie, and I used to go to a Toronto Maple Leafs game with the Duracell group. The evening started at the Hot Stove Lounge, and we then headed up to Duracell's corporate box. On one of those Saturday nights, we were asked to stop by the Pepsi box for a drink. By the time we arrived, we were pretty much in the bag.

The sales manager (who nobody liked) offered me a drink, and I replied, "I'll have a rum and Coke," which was my standard drink in those days.

"A rum and what?" he asked. Having been told to be on my best behavior, I politely repeated my order: "I'll have a rum and Coke, please," not catching my faux pas. Then he kept asking me over and over in his condescending way, "a rum and what, a rum and what?" Finally, I'd had enough of his attitude and asked him if he was "fucking deaf." That's when all hell broke loose. Johnny would, as usual, play diplomat, apologize for my behavior, and get me my rum and Pepsi.

This type of thing happened all the time. I'd say something inappropriate to someone, and Johnny, Dan, or Lennie would jump in and save the day. As you can imagine, this dynamic didn't endear me to whoever was on the other side of my brashness.

I think I'm blind in one eye

One night, Brad, Dan, Johnny, and the rest of the crowd went to the Rodeo, a popular bar in Moncton, on a mission to spend as much of the company's money as we could. On the way home, six of us stuffed ourselves into a cab where Brad and I started play-fighting. Of course, it got a little rougher than intended, and Brad scratched my face.

We had a big meeting the next day. In the morning, when I got up, I put on my glasses to inspect the scratch and realized that I couldn't see anything out of my left eye. I said to myself, "The bastard must have poked me in the eye." Now I was really pissed off. Well, until I realized that the lens from my glasses was missing; my eye was fine.

I collected myself and headed down to the corporate event. The meeting was well underway when I arrived. As I opened the door, my colleagues took one look at my sorry ass (hungover, disheveled, with a ten-inch scratch down my face), and the room instantly erupted in laughter. The outburst was so out of control that the meeting had to be adjourned to give everyone time to catch their breath.

That was our environment. We played hard and were proud of it. We all knew, or at least had ourselves convinced, that the fun we shared and the bond we created was the key to our success. As I look back many years later, I am sure it was. After all, we were leading the country by almost every operational measurement.

Often, my work friends comingled with my other friends at our annual neighborhood beach party. The party was officially on Saturday, yet, most years, to my wife's dismay, it started on Friday night. On one of those pre-party nights, there were only eight of us, but we were noisy. Monique, who was trying to sleep, had had enough of our foolishness. She summoned me to our room, where she made it clear that I must "get them to quiet down or die."

I have to admit that she pushed all the right buttons that night and had me rattled. I stormed down to the outside bar where the boys were playing guitar and singing, and I firmly told them to quiet down. They, of course, ignored me. But I knew the noise had to stop; my life depended on it. So, I started getting more aggressive, but they just kept laughing at me.

My friend Rob started mocking me, like Elmer Fudd, , "be very, very, quiet" and the laughter became even louder. Meanwhile, I knew Monique was sharpening her knives upstairs.

I started yelling, "Shut the fuck up!" I was starting to lose it. Then, another friend named Rod got up to tell the boys to quiet down and accidentally kicked over a garbage can full of bottles and cans, making more noise. Then he tried to pick them up, kicking them everywhere in the process, making even more noise. It was the drunk-guy domino effect in full colour.

By this point, I was losing my mind. I could feel the veins in my neck about to burst. Dan, in his drunken state, came over and told me he didn't mean it. He was pleading with me to understand that he was not causing trouble on purpose, and then, for some unknown reason, he slapped me hard.

I was in shock. The place went quiet. I looked around me and grabbed the closest object, the plastic lid of the garbage can, and hit him square in the beak, causing him to stumble backward. I hit him again, and he cartwheeled ass over teakettle. The place was in full commotion: half went bug-eyed in shock, and the rest were laughing uncontrollably.

It took some time, but I finally got them to quiet down, put some ice on Dan's face, and then reluctantly went back up to the she-devil's den. When she first complained, it was noisy, but while I was down there, it was deafening! When I arrived at the room, she looked like Linda Blair in *The Exorcist*; her head was spinning 360 degrees with lightning bolts shooting out of every orifice. It was bloody scary! I somehow managed to physically survive the ordeal, but I was emotionally scarred forever.

From that day forward, we all knew not to mess around with Monique when she was ready for bed. As a prize for her part in the evening, she was baptized with the nickname 'Noise Nazi.'

Creating the conditions for success

Dan would continue to offer me words of advice, with a keen sense of how my team and customers were feeling about my leadership, which would prove to be invaluable as I moved into my executive years. As my career at SDM continued, I became the sales manager for our private-label brand.

The new job involved working with the folks in the Toronto office, who were a different breed: more conservative, self-centered, and by the book. Yet, I managed to find a few like myself among them. John Gamble, VP of Marketing, was one of those characters. He was funny, charming, smart, and of course, loved to have a drink. We worked together on various product rollouts and even spent a weekend flying around Eastern Canada on the Cott Beverages' corporate jet, drinking rum and Coke, or I should say rum and Life Brand cola, while the stores were doing tastings of Life Brand cola, Coke, and Pepsi. (We won.)

John Gamble, Dan and I once visited St. John's, Newfoundland, where the local stores decided they wanted to 'Screech' John G. in. 'Screeching in' is a Newfoundland tradition that makes you an honorary Newfoundlander. It consists of saying a rhyme as you chug Screech (Newfoundland rum), preceded by kissing a cod. The Newfoundland group loved conducting the ceremony and always made it quite a spectacle. John G. did his part, got through the rhyme, kissed the cod, and drank the rum. As a gift, the group gave him a twelve-pack of Screech travel bottles.

John G., who had been a little nervous before the ceremony, was now feeling pretty good about his performance and proceeded to drink most of the twelve-pack. After putting down about ten mini-bottles, his body moved like it was a well-cooked noodle. We tried to take him to a few bars on George Street, but without functioning motor skills, he didn't make it far. So, we took him back to the hotel, where we asked the desk for a key to his room. They refused, saying, "We can only give it to the occupant of the room," as if the bastard wasn't right in front of them. We replied, "He's right here." They said, "He's not awake."

We quickly got tired of arguing, so we said, "Okay, you keep him," and walked away, leaving him passed out on the couch. Within seconds, the key was in our hands, and they were begging us to take the wet noodle to his room.

Over and over, the same thing kept happening; we bonded with the people we had fun with, which caused us to work together more effectively, allowing things to get done like never before. This resulted in our 'Life Brand' sales penetration doubling that of any other region in the country.

Times were good, sales were up, and we were having fun, but as it happens in any company, things started to change, people came and went, and the environment hardened.

Look for the silver linings

Despite my top-tier performance, hitting double-digit sales and profit growth, penetration levels, and after blowing the top off team engagement levels, I was axed.

Yep, a major restructuring eliminated the director-level positions across the country. Of course, the fat that should have been trimmed was the highest-salaried VPs and Senior VPs, but they were calling the shots. They weren't going to eliminate themselves.

That's the way it works. You've been warned. The best security against this is staying true to yourself and developing your unique set of skills; twisting and contorting yourself into becoming what the company wants won't save you.

That said, I ended up feeling okay about the layoff. After all, the entire team dynamic had changed, and my chances of moving up the ladder were next to zero as a non-pharmacist. And there was a silver lining. Within weeks of my leaving Shoppers, I was sitting in the office of a recruiter for McKesson, which marked the beginning of a new chapter in my life. Oh, and by the way, Harry, who had carried out his orders with such enthusiasm, was terminated only a few months later by the very same Senior VPs he was trying so hard to please. Karma's a bitch!

Luckily for me, a friend of my wife's who was leaving his position at McKesson recommended me to his boss, Dale Weil, and the interview process began. The executive search was coordinated through a headhunter who just happened to be Monique's former boss. The interviews went well, and I seemed to have a strong connection with Dale. However, I knew from my past experiences that the testing component of the interview process would be the stumbling block. I explained my learning disabilities to the headhunter and showed him my psychological evaluation, which he then explained to McKesson.

With a great deal of understanding, trust, and solid support from my industry colleagues, I was able to get the job. In July 2000, I started my new career with McKesson Canada, taking the lead role in Atlantic Canada. The opportunity this role afforded me was truly exciting: I would be able to manage the entire Atlantic regional team my way.

I loved my years at Shoppers. I became an expert on how to operate pharmacies, create profit, and control expenses. More importantly, I learned a lot about myself and what I had to offer. It was clear to me that we excelled the most as a team when we were having the most fun. From the fun spun the relationships and an unbreakable bond that set us apart from other teams.

Sadly, I would also experience the collapse of a great team as new bosses forced their will, operating style, and culture on the team. The environment would slowly harden and crumble, people would leave, and what had been a great team would be all but a faint memory. The reality is that a business unit is just a collection of people. Whether they become a team will have everything to do with their leader's approach. Be that person!

Key takeaways

- A relaxed fun-filled environment drives performance.
- Twisting and contorting yourself into something you're not will make you less efficient.
- When the joy in your work is gone, find another place to work.

LESSON 11

Leave enough room for the possibility that you don't know shit

The only barrier to truth is the presumption that you already have it.

Chuck Missler

After I got my psychological test results and realized how I was making 'being me' work, I felt like I was at the top of my game. Out of nowhere, I had gotten a job in retail pharma, risen through the ranks, lost that job, and then, out of the blue again, landed another job many would have killed for. On top of that, I was working with people I loved and was married with two wonderful children. Frankly, I was on top of the world. All I needed was a reality check, and, oh boy, would I get one. The lesson I needed to learn at this point in my life would come in the shape of a very ill-fated maritime adventure.

Voyage from hell

When we were living in Glen Haven, on the shores of St. Margaret's Bay, Nova Scotia, we had an adventure that taught me a very important lesson. In case you've never heard of it, St. Margaret's Bay is a beautiful community just outside of Halifax, celebrated as one of the best boating areas in that part of the world. After we moved to our new ocean playground, we decided that we needed a boat—a boat capable of handling these ocean waters, accommodating our group of friends, and with enough room for my wife to sunbathe.

We agreed that a used fishing boat would fit the bill. After scouring the countryside, I found a well-used, forty-two-foot Cape Islander named The Corey in Tignish, Prince Edward Island. To get the boat home, we had to sail it along the north coast of the island, across St. George's bay through the Canso Canal, between Cape Breton and mainland Nova Scotia (passing through Chedabucto Bay), down the east coast of Nova Scotia by Halifax Harbour and Peggy's Cove, and on to St. Margaret's Bay and home.

I easily recruited three sailors to join me. It was going to be fun, fun, fun—an adventure to remember. I mean, who *wouldn't* want to go? Sailor number one was Doug Smith, a good buddy of mine, a real outdoorsman, and the best party guy I knew, so he was a must. Sailor number two was Fraser Morrison, a nice guy who worked for one of our suppliers. He was a great handyman and a seasoned boater with years of experience on Bras d'Or Lake in Cape Breton. Sailor number three, Gordon McEwen, who worked with me at Shoppers Drug Mart, was our MacGyver, capable of fixing almost anything.

In preparation for our voyage, Gordon and I traveled to Tignish the weekend before to ready the boat. As we did, the locals stopped and watched us from the wharf above. They never spoke, just peered down at us in the oddest way. Gordon and I thought, *man, they're weird.* In hindsight, they must have thought our plan to sail the North Atlantic on one long weekend in May, in an old boat, and with little experience was whacked! Little did they know that in preparation for the trip, I had taken loads of boating courses: basic boating, safety, and navigation. So, while I might have been light on experience, I was loaded up with 'book knowledge.' *I got this*, I thought.

When we arrived at the wharf on the morning of our departure, we joined the hustle and bustle of dozens of fishermen heading out to sea for the day. We loaded the beer, the cooler full of lobster, and other goodies, and we were ready to go. As I turned the key to start the boat, there wasn't a flicker of life. After some tinkering, we figured out that the battery was dead. We mustered up a new one and finally got on our way.

It was a glorious morning; the sun was shining and the water smooth. It was exactly what we were hoping for. We cruised for about six hours without a care in the world. We had a few beers, laughed, told jokes, and enjoyed the marvelous coastline, thinking about how blessed we were to be part of this adventure. As we reached the northern end of the island and turned into the head of St. George's Bay, the water conditions roughened. Inexperienced as we were, we decided to change course and head to Souris, Prince Edward Island, for the night.

'Any time you are ready, captain!'

As we pulled up to the dock, it began to rain. It wouldn't stop for the next three days, and as a special bonus, the temperature would drop to eight degrees Celsius. The next morning, we crossed St. George's Bay, which we had cowardly retreated from the day before. Now, with one more day of experience, we handled the crossing with ease. What a team!

I radioed the Canso Canal operator, informing him that we were coming into the canal. They opened the first lock, and we entered. Then, to complete the process, the canal operator had to swing the bridge, stopping the traffic, and open the second gate. We were then supposed to exit the canal. That's when we encountered the second issue with our boat: the gear shift froze, and with the strong currents in the canal, the boat began to float aimlessly. Gordon flew into action. He took the gear shift apart and MacGyvered it as best he could.

So, here's the scene: The bridge was fully swung open, boat traffic was lined up for miles, and we were sideways in the canal. At this very moment, the canal operator said over the radio, in the most sarcastic voice possible: "Anytime. . . you're. . . ready. . . captain!" Immediately, Gordon got the gear shift back together. We straightened out the boat and motored out of the canal, which was a challenge with my crew rolling on the floor, laughing uncontrollably over the canal operator's timely comment! Those words, "Anytime you're ready, captain," would be repeated a thousand times for many years to come as a reminder of our trip, which was still a long way from over.

Once we were finally out of the canal, we motored by Port Hawkesbury and sailed toward Chedabucto Bay. As we entered the bay, the waters were pretty good, but soon enough, we experienced the roughest water yet. At that point, we decided to reverse course, heading back to Port Hawkesbury, where we spent the night tied up to the provincial wharf. The weather still sucked. It was cold and rainy. Everyone was grumpy and uncomfortable; the crew was not exactly having the fun they had signed up for. The next morning, we were all feeling better, rested, and ready to go. When we got to the point where we had turned around the previous day, the weather conditions seemed more reasonable. However, by the time we got to the middle of the bay, it felt like we were in a hurricane, and our boat was being tossed around by fifteen-foot waves, with every fifth wave an absolute monster. The waves were hitting the boat so hard that the water sprayed through the planks at the bow.

I think I'm going to die

The crew was scared shitless. We thought we were going to die. As each monster wave slammed into the boat, all I could hear was, "Here it comes... here it comes... get ready... get readyyyy. Bang... crash... Oh, shit... Oh, shit... Woo... Is everyone okay? Okay! Let's get ready for the next one!" The waves were so big that our only option was to go straight ahead. If we tried to make the turn back to Port Hawkesbury, the boat would most likely capsize, so there was no escaping the torture.

The crew was so frantic by this point that they wanted to run the boat aground and take their chances. I convinced them that was crazy talk; the rocky shoreline would tear us apart. Remember, this was in May, and the waters were freezing. Should we tumble into the sea, wearing our life jackets would only prolong our agony. I must admit that if someone had offered me ten bucks and a safe passage home at that moment, I would have grabbed it in a heartbeat.

As we were being pounded by the seas, my job was to make sure we stayed on course. As rough as it was, the even greater danger was getting off course and hitting one of those rocky shoals that were scattered throughout the bay.

I was trying to navigate, but as each big wave hit the boat, I went flying, only to get back up and try to keep plotting our course. When we finally came to the mouth of the bay and turned to travel south along the Nova Scotia coastline, it was like a miracle. The waters turned into a smooth-flowing sea, and the pounding finally stopped. The look of relief on everyone's face was quite a sight. We continued down the coast, had a couple of beers, smoked a joint, and came to an agreement not to abandon ship after all.

The situation we had just experienced was nothing like what I had learned in the classroom. My charts were wet, and the pencil would tear through the paper. There was no level or dry surface to work on, and I was being thrown around like a ragdoll. This was in addition to the stress and anxiety that consumed both captain and crew. At that exact moment, I had a damning revelation: My perception of what was required for a successful trip and the reality of the situation were light-years apart. It was a lesson I wouldn't forget for the rest of my life. Yet, our voyage was still far from over.

We decided to take advantage of the calmer waters and refuel the boat. I had Doug take the wheel while Fraser, Gordon, and I transferred the diesel from the extra fuel barrel to the boat's fuel tank. I set the boat on a heading; everything looked clear. Doug's job was to keep looking out and keep us on course until we were done refueling. That's when the boys decided to tell me about the third issue with our boat. It seemed that one of the fuel lines had sprung a leak. Thank God for good ol'

Gordon, who once again jumped into action and repaired the line—well, at least good enough to get us home.

Then, out of nowhere, bang! The three of us went flying across the deck in different directions. "What the hell happened?" one of the guys yelled. As we got to our feet, all we could see through the windshield were rocks, fucking mountains of rocks. We couldn't believe our eyes! We started yelling at Doug, "Didn't you see the goddamn rock island?" Doug answered, "Yes, but you told me to stay on this heading." Can you imagine? We all gave him an earful, but it seemed that the boat was okay, so our verbal assault quickly turned into laughter.

The stress and excitement of the last few days had been exhausting, and the idea of sleeping another night in the wet, cold boat was less than appealing. So, we decided to pull into a small town along the coast, called for a fuel truck, booked rooms at a local motel, and hired a taxi to take our sorry asses to the comfort of a warm bed.

Steady-as-she-goes. . . Not!

The room felt like heaven: warm and dry. I jumped into a hot shower and then into bed. It felt amazing. We all had a great sleep, grabbed a bite to eat, and got a cab to take us back to the boat. When we arrived, the boat was still tied to the dock, just as we had left it. While nobody said it, I am sure we were all wishing our vessel from hell had sunk during the night. No such luck, so onboard we went for our last leg of the journey—across the mouth of Halifax Harbour, Peggy's Cove, and into St. Margaret's Bay and home. The ocean was calm, the rain had stopped, and the fog had come in, giving us limited visibility.

I knew that going into the fog without radar had its risks, but after what we had gone through, nobody cared. We moved through the water at ease and cruised for about three hours. As we moved toward the entrance to Halifax Harbour, I contacted the harbour master and advised him of our position, speed, and course. "You're on course, and your speed is fine," he replied. "Steady-as-she-goes!" He also gave us the locations of other vessels in the area. These included two U.S. Navy destroyers—one of them anchored in the mouth of the harbour, the other one coming out—and a container ship coming into the mouth. We were good to go and had done everything by the book. Radar would have been nice, but we had the comfort of having been given the 'all okay.'

We stayed tuned to the Halifax Harbour frequency, and a few minutes later, we heard the U.S. Navy destroyer contact the container ship and advise it that it was not on course. The container ship captain insisted that it was on course. At that point, the destroyer captain made it clear that the container ship was in violation of international law and needed to alter course immediately. If not, the destroyer would take action. Then it just got nasty.

The fog was thick, with approximately 100 feet of visibility. I quickly realized this couldn't be good and got everyone out on the deck, looking in different directions for any movement. Then we heard this weird sound: whoosh. . . whoosh. . . whoosh. . . whoosh. It kept getting louder. Then someone yelled, "I think I see something coming!" Then, through the fog, we saw a giant 'V' shape. It was the bow of the massive container ship coming through the fog. Everyone started yelling. "Gunner! Move it! Get out of here!" We hit the gas and pushed the boat as fast as it would go. Almost miraculously, the container ship passed to our stern by about fifty feet.

We couldn't help but look at each other in total disbelief. We were all thinking, *How much shit can go wrong on this goddamn trip?* Pissed off, I called the harbour master to complain. He had zero sympathy for our predicament and quickly put me in my place for being out there without radar.

We passed through the rest of the mouth of the harbour without incident, past world-famous Peggy's Cove, and then into St. Margaret's Bay, to Glen Haven, and home.

We had all called our wives to let them know when we were arriving, but none of us had shared many details about the voyage. As we arrived at the dock, our families were there with banners and balloons, welcoming home the great adventurers! As we shuffled off the boat, they could see that our mood didn't quite match their expectations. We shared a short version of our tale but were so exhausted, both mentally and physically, that we all just wanted to go to bed. The story of this trip has been told many times over the years, and we've had many a laugh about our voyage from hell.

Thanks to this experience, I learned one hell of a lesson in humility. Everything that transpired over the course of those four days cemented in my mind the firm belief that no matter how sure I might be about my abilities, how committed I might be to my direction, or how solid I may think my facts are, I should always leave enough room for the possibility that I don't know shit!

Leo Tolstoy once said, "Perfection is impossible without humility. Why should I strive for perfection if I am already good enough?" I understand now that if I hadn't been so sure of myself, our trip would probably have been much less problematic. Like the best among us, I had to go through tremendous hardship to learn that one cannot strive for perfection without humility. From those hellish roaring seas, I emerged with the wisdom that comes from accepting that you might not know much at all—and that's alright.

As I pondered my new sense of humility, I realized that I had been the boss of some group of people or another for countless years, which made my jokes the funniest, my solutions the best, and my personality a mix between Indiana Jones, Alfred Einstein, and Brad Pitt—ha! Of course, it's not real, but it made me understand why most managers have inflated egos.

That is the dilemma. If you accept my assumption that humility is a leader's greatest asset, how do you stay humble with so much unwarranted praise flowing in your direction? Taking risks, pushing your limits, and failing regularly certainly help. Hanging with your family and surrounding yourself with people willing and able to convey to you the hard realities about your shortcomings is pretty much essential.

The lesson on humility I learned on that boat trip was life-altering. Wondering if I was going to die because of my arrogance would cause me to reevaluate our thinking.

Equipped with my new sense of humility, I would pour more and more responsibility onto my team, letting go of control, forcing them to run with the ball, and encouraging them to be aggressive and unafraid of making a mistake. The result was a new level of performance and growth in team engagement. My voyage through hell and the lessons learned brought me closer to true leadership. So, my advice is to pack your ego away and find humility!

Key takeaways

- Humility is essential to leadership and comes from owning your mistakes, so be unafraid of making a few.
- Your perception of events and reality may be very different; acknowledge that, learn from it, and move on.

LESSON 12

Find leadership experiences outside of work

Never say never because limits, like fears, are often just illusions.

Michael Jordan

Learning to embrace my limitations and the importance of humility were two big ones for me. Without the experiences that led to internalizing those beliefs, my career might well have taken a less-than-stellar path. Over the next period of my life, I would reconnect with my passion for coaching, learn about the importance of losing, and reflect on the intricacies of decision-making. I would also understand that being the favorite is rarely an advantage, that goals and achievements must be measured in context, and that being yourself is the solution to many a conundrum. Most of these lessons would be learned outside of the workplace—leading athletes toward victory while doing one of the things I loved most.

What the hell is Ringette?

Once upon a time, coaching was my world; it was the only thing I seemed to be good at. It instilled in me a sense of pride and self-worth that I'd never had before. After my initial coaching successes, I even took my second degree at Concordia in pursuit of my coaching dream. Then, life took over, and my desire to coach was eclipsed by my short-term need to find a job and my unquenchable thirst for a good time.

When I was offered the job at Pharmaprix—having zero cash and no prospects of a job or foreseeable coaching opportunities—I grabbed it and never looked back. Little by little, my dream of coaching faded into a distant memory, at least for a while.

When I was forty-three, after fourteen years of marriage, my four-year-old daughter Jessica came to me and asked if she could play Ringette. "What's Ringette?" I asked. Essentially, for those who don't know, it's played on ice, with a rubber ring and a hockey stick with no blade. The objective of the game is to put the ring in the other team's net. My Ringette friends would kill me for describing it this way, but never mind. It is a fantastic sport, fast and exciting, with tens of thousands of girls playing across Canada and many more around the world.

Puppy points

So, off to the rink we went, and my daughter loved it, especially when we played games. Well, to be clear, what she loved was skating aimlessly up and down the ice, often stopping to chat with the other team's goalie while the game raged on the other side of the rink. Though she had become a great skater, she had no interest in scoring, getting involved in plays, or even going for the ring. While other parents marveled at her advanced skating skills, my wife and I would only nod and smile, not wanting to be politically incorrect, while thinking, *Will you just touch the ring, please? There's a game going on here!*

While Jessica's lack of competitiveness was cute in a way, it was a little embarrassing for her Type-A parents. In our eyes, at the time, being good parents meant ensuring our daughter grew up to be a strong, assertive woman who knew how to take charge, which in this case meant get the damn ring! Eventually, we came up with a plan, not for her to score goals or even carry the ring; we just wanted her to touch it. She had been begging us for a puppy for months, so we told her she could earn puppy points by merely touching the ring. One hundred touches meant one hundred points and a new puppy.

Based on her past performances, we thought it would take her a year. It was at that moment that we first experienced her dogged determination to get what she wanted. After we made our 'deal,' as soon as her little feet hit the ice, she was flying around like a madwoman. After only a few games, she had her one hundred points, and we were begrudgingly off to pick up her new puppy. Over the years, we have been accused of essentially bribing our child to perform instead of just letting her have fun. But that just wasn't the way we saw it at the time. We hadn't interfered with the coach or team, her new attitude didn't cause her to have less fun, and she was tremendously proud of her accomplishment.

Rediscovering a lost love

In those early years, when I took Jessica to the rink, I often went on the ice to help out behind the bench and quickly became intrigued with the idea of maybe coaching again. I thought I might be able to do a good job. I had the success and experience of the swim team coaching under my belt, I had been successfully managing and motivating people throughout my career, and I was a pretty skilled organizer. Most importantly, I learned how to win, which I thought could be easily transferred back to sports. Who doesn't want to win?

When I leaped back into coaching, I also brought with me a certain perspective. I believed that sports should emulate life, and it was important for kids to learn about the right combination of fun, hard work, and accountability. I didn't believe in the participation-medal culture. I thought it was okay for kids to experience losing; that's life! I believed that dealing with loss in a positive, constructive manner was a vital skill for them to develop.

I also brought with me a basket of other interesting personality traits. I was stubborn and pigheaded, sometimes insensitive, sometimes too sensitive, straightforward, and always prepared to stand my ground with anyone who might challenge my thinking. I often heard parents say that the kids "only want to have fun," and I generally agreed. However, our divergent definitions of fun made all the difference. In my mind, a girl who works her ass off in practice is having just as much fun as the girl making snow angels in the corner. Two girls, same game, and two very different perspectives on what constitutes fun.

I came to realize that parenting roles were shifting. When I coached the swim team, I never saw a parent. Hell, that's why they put them on the team; they were just happy to get them out of the house for a couple of hours. In this new world, 'helicopter parents' flooded the arenas, ready to protect their children against any perceived injustice. In many cases, they fundamentally believed it was their right to be part of the team's decision-making process. That was never going to fly with me. If you have eighteen kids on the team, you have at least eighteen parents, each looking at the game through the eye of their child, which gives them a very singular perspective rather than a broader team outlook.

Losing perspective

As a coach, I always tried to balance everyone's diverse wants and needs as best I could. Yet, my self-centeredness, need for control, stubbornness, and burning desire to win would inevitably lead me down shit's creek more than once.

A couple of years into my Ringette coaching, we went to the house league provincial championships with no real hope of winning. Next thing we knew, we had unexpectedly advanced to the championship game—a total shocker!

My mind quickly went to, *How can I capitalize on this opportunity?* In my self-centered worldview, that could only mean one thing: *How can I win?*

I held a meeting with the players and coaches (no parents) and proceeded to pitch to a group of ten-year-old girls the idea of cutting the bench in order to win, explaining that it was probably the only way we could earn the title.

The girls agreed, and the next day, we came out flying, unfortunately losing by one goal in the last minute. Silver medal! Pretty good considering what our expectations were a few days earlier.

Yet, that wasn't the vibe I was getting from anyone. No one seemed happy about our accomplishment. The girls who hadn't played felt left out and abandoned, the girls who had played were upset at the perceived injustice to their teammates, and then there were the fire-breathing parents, who were ready to hang me from the highest tree. It was a total disaster, and I went from good old coach to public enemy number one in the hour it took to play the game.

In the end, I survived my error in judgment and accepted that my decision-making had been ill-advised; benching a group of young kids who I deemed to be less talented to secure my legacy wasn't my best look. My desire to win had overpowered my sense of right and wrong. The reality was that the girls were too young to make an informed decision. I had used my considerable powers of persuasion to convince the other coaches to do it my way and had only consulted the Rick-friendly parents.

The experience and the aftermath of the championship weekend taught me another lesson in humility, one that would prompt me to examine my motives before making decisions. I also understood that my coaching style was probably better suited for a more competitive environment.

The problem was that there was no competitive team for girls of this age. I was determined to keep coaching, so I took the bull by the horns and lobbied the Southeast Ringette Association to form a new competitive team. After some debate, I was given the green light. The team would be called "The Freeze," and I would be its first head coach. As I entered this new world, I knew I needed to have the right people around me, the kind who could counterbalance my tendency to make rash, selfish decisions.

I had worked successfully with Rob and Sandra Raftus in the Riverview Association, so they were a must. Then I added Paul Poirier, who brought a more logical, more common approach and who spoke French, allowing him to communicate better with the French-speaking players.

Understanding who's on your team

Our main objective was to ensure that the parents were informed and engaged. I had learned, like it or not, that parents were, for all intents and purposes, part of the team. So, in an attempt to create just the right chemistry, we spent considerable time communicating, laying out our plans, and getting the parents involved in fundraising and other activities. At the same time, we made it clear to them that we didn't want them involved in the team's on-ice operations. Thankfully, they agreed and, for the most part, stayed true to their word.

What followed was an endless list of team activities, bus rides, board games, camping trips, team sleepovers, fishing excursions, and fundraising events. At each tournament, we booked a hospitality (party) room, where some kind of foolishness usually took place, causing parents to do stupid things like sliding down snowy hills on the hotel ironing boards and the like. We were having a ball, and our many planned and unplanned escapades ended up creating a very special bond, one that would be crowned by two Provincial and Atlantic Championship victories in two consecutive years.

Coming off these fun and gratifying years, I was excited about my third year coaching the elite team. However, I was about to receive a wake-up call about how things worked in the cutthroat world of community minor sports.

I have spent decades dealing with slimy executives and battling narcissistic, sociopathic businessmen, but nothing in this world compares to the agony of community minor sports and the ridiculous politics. It comes from the parents. Every single one believes they know what's best and, by God, they all have the next little 'superstar' to protect. Managing the endless barrage of conflicting interests of blinded-by-love parents is like running through a field of bloodthirsty zombies.

The decision as to who would coach the teams was decided by a vote. This process was carried out by the Southeast Association board (made up of parents), with each community getting an equal vote. With the influx of new communities and their respective representatives (parents again), they voted to give the team to another coach. I thought, *This is impossible! I am the most qualified and successful coach by a mile.* The elected candidate didn't even have the minimum qualifications to apply for the role, let alone to actually coach the team. Yet, nothing mattered except that show of hands.

It was another reminder that life's not fair! Getting a job often has nothing to do with your ability or preparedness but with who you know, political agendas, timing, and pure luck. I'd have to reluctantly suck it up!

My daughter and many of my past players tried out and made the team, and then to my surprise, I received a call from the new coach, whose name was Leon, asking me if I would help him coach the team. I knew Leon's reputation, so there was no way I could join the team as an assistant coach and be a slave to his coaching philosophy. After some discussion, we agreed that I would come on board as a co-coach with equal responsibilities.

Making the best of a bad situation

The year turned out to be quite an experience, filled with conflicting points of view and lots of drama. The team would never recapture the magic that we'd had in previous years, yet we still managed to win our third consecutive Provincial and Atlantic championships, as well as a silver medal at the Eastern Championships. Nevertheless, my co-coaching experience with someone more foe than friend was challenging. From the beginning, I knew I'd have to compromise if 'the girls' had any hope of having an experience close to what they deserved.

It was hard at times. Leon's approach and focus seemed counterintuitive to mine and didn't always seem to be in the best interest of the team. Thank God Rob was there to calm me down, give me a more positive take on things, and ultimately convince me not to 'accidentally' push Leon in front of the Zamboni.

As the new year began, I was back at it with a different group of girls. I was still coaching my daughter Jessica, who alternated between two age groups. In their first year in an age group, the girls were more focused on their social life, while the parents were more protective and sensitive to their children's needs and wants. The second year, the kids were more focused on playing Ringette, while their parents were more in line with my accountability and hard-work approach, resulting in less drama.

By now, I understood quite well that parents were an unavoidable part of the team; their attitudes and actions influenced their children. In this particular year, the parents happened to be great, the kids performed well and won the Provincial and Atlantic Championships, and then we were off to the Eastern Championships.

In this final challenge, Quebec was the team to beat. They were an absolute powerhouse. I had to admit that they were fun to watch. They were killing everyone in the tournament. They had crushed Nova Scotia in the prelims and seemed pretty much unbeatable. Luckily for us, we didn't have to face them until the semifinals. I knew the Quebec coach was an over-the-top-confident type of guy. I was sure he had likely passed this overconfidence on to his team, and I was hoping it would be their ultimate downfall.

I learned many times over the years that being the favorite is rarely an advantage. Regardless of how much you tell yourself not to be overconfident, it's incredibly hard to keep that flame burning in your belly. We had trained for these exact circumstances. No other team was in better physical condition, and we had mastered the skills and tactics required in this situation. It was one game, and we only had to outplay them for sixty minutes. Our plan was simple: We had to aggressively take away their time and space.

Our girls came out flying, swarming them like bees to honey. The Quebec players couldn't move, and we took command of the game, eliminating them from the competition. It was a tremendous effort and probably the best game we ever played. The winner of the other semifinal was Nova Scotia, whom we had just beaten a few weeks earlier in the Atlantic Championships, so they'd be hungry. I knew that could play to our disadvantage if we didn't come out fast and aggressive.

Unfortunately, as the semis began, I lost the services of my all-star defensive player, who was accidentally given the wrong dosage of medication, which made her incapable of playing. It was a monumental loss; Erica was a key to our success. Without her, it was going to be difficult, and the girls knew it. Nonetheless, we again came out flying and quickly took a commanding three-goal lead. Then something happened; I could see it in their eyes. It was like they hit a wall. The effort of beating Quebec, losing Erica, and the pressure of the week, added to the team's inexperience, had taken its toll. I called a timeout with a two-goal lead and tried as best I could to take the pressure off, but I could sense the girls were emotionally drained. Nova Scotia went on to erase our lead and win the title.

Understanding what success looks like

It was disappointing, but I couldn't be prouder. What an outstanding performance by our girls! They had beaten the best team and played their best game. What more could one ask? It was a fun and successful year. I learned a lot from the tournament, especially the last two games. We had trained hard for this championship, and we executed our plan faultlessly. Unfortunately, sometimes shit happens, and the prize eludes you. That's life!

Our success was impressive. It was the first time for most of the girls to compete in the Eastern Championship. And yet, they came within a hair of winning it all. This experience taught me that great teams aren't always defined by wins and losses. I couldn't help but connect this experience to my work, where the success of a business unit is usually based on making your numbers, regardless of whether you achieved it through hard work or just shithouse luck.

Countless times in my career, I have seen a team encounter obstacle after obstacle totally out of their control and fall short of their numbers. Meanwhile, another team that got all the breaks or sandbagged their numbers is seen as a superior performer. I am not suggesting that results or winning aren't important (I think I've illustrated that by now), but a sole focus on these measurements can serve to disguise failing businesses and poor leadership.

Flawed or not, I'm at my best when I'm me

As my fifth year approached, I wasn't sure I wanted to coach. My children were getting into other activities, and our top players had moved on. But it was the first year the girls were eligible to go to the Nationals, and a number of parents were encouraging me to take at least one shot at it. However, having been involved in minor sports for years, dealing with parents and associations had worn me down. I just didn't have the energy to keep fighting all sides. And with Leon and his cohorts of parents coming back into the fold, I wasn't sure I could bear the torture.

To try and ease my pain, I decided to adjust my coaching style. I would try to be more accommodating, roll more with the punches, and generally be more relaxed about things. My new approach, a complete contrast to my instincts, seemed to work at first. But as the year went on, one compromise led to another, and it became clear that my new, easy-going style wasn't having the intended effect. But by then, the horse was out of the barn, so I had to grit my teeth and carry on. After muddling our way to our fifth consecutive Provincial and Atlantic Championships, we got to the final, where we beat Nova Scotia, a team against which we had lost every game during the season.

Winning when it matters

The one thing I had been able to do successfully over the years was winning when it mattered. We developed a system that identified a few specific goals and a game plan that solely focused on achieving those goals on specific dates. We learned to turn our losses into a powerful tool. We used the lessons of our defeats to identify our weaknesses and adjust our practice plan accordingly. Then we funneled our learning into those moments when winning was essential to meeting our goals. Based on this formula, regardless of all the dissension and mayhem, the girls still performed well, though regrettably not with the same passion and joy they might have experienced in a more cohesive environment.

After we won the Atlantic Championship, the same opinionated parents who usually found fault were over-the-top excited about our victory. As they celebrated, they threw heaps of praise my way, telling me I had done "such an amazing job," while I just smiled, amazed at how brilliant I had become all of a sudden. As I listened to these parents celebrate, there was a clear sense of finality to their words, and I knew that for all practical purposes, our season was over, and our trip to the Nationals would be a sham. Of course, I tried to refocus the team, but by then, the negative forces had derailed any sense of commitment to our goals, and I'd have to admit that for the first time in my adult life. During my week at the Nationals, I gave up, pulled in my horns, and escaped into myself, a situation I vowed would never happen again.

After these experiences, I learned that trying to be something I am not and ignoring my instincts robbed me of what made me effective. It may have played to the benefit of a few but did not maximize the potential of the team.

No more Mr. Sensitive

Soon after our dismal performance at the Nationals, Gilles Maltais, a parent whose daughter had played on my teams for years, told me, "You only caused yourself grief when you started listening to parents, trying to be Mister Sensitive. You should have stayed the course of the old Rick Brennan, the one who didn't give a crap what anyone thought, did your thing, and took no shit. That's when you and your team truly excelled." His words were a wake-up call and reminded me that regardless of how 'imperfect' I might be, being 'me' was at the core of my success.

The paradox of winning

I was lucky in my Ringette coaching career, winning five Provincial and Atlantic Championships and two silver medals at the Eastern Championships over a period of five years. Yet, if I'm honest, I don't think that every team was great or that I exhibited the leadership qualities required in every situation. Leading people can be hard; outside forces, opposing agendas, and emotions can make it almost impossible to get everyone moving in the same direction.

Yet, our systems were so well-rehearsed, our physical conditioning so strong, and our goals so entrenched in the team's mindset that the team always performed well, especially when it mattered.

In the end, and as crazy as it sounds, the victories that we chased so relentlessly were never as fulfilling as I had anticipated. Sure, we'd yell, jump up and down, do the hugs-and-kisses thing, but usually, I'd just sigh in relief, happy not to have screwed it up. I got into Ringette to be closer to my daughter, and we spent a lot of time together over the years. She has nothing but fond memories; gotta be happy with that!

As I continued in my business career, my coaching experiences gave me a reference point and an understanding of teamwork, people, and leadership that most other executives lacked. As I tried to put together my work teams, I used this knowledge to inform my search for people with similar values and perspectives—people who had the skills that I lacked and personalities and operating styles in tune with my own.

Looking back, I now see that there is no way in hell I could have acquired this vital wisdom if I had stuck to focusing on leadership in the workplace. Coaching sports gave me a perspective that would be invaluable over the years.

Pick your team with great care; disruptive forces within a team can stifle performance and suck the fun out of the environment. If you're the boss, hold people accountable not just for their operational performance and financial results but for their attitude and interaction with other team members. This can be difficult, so talk to your team up front and clearly identify what the 'right' attitude looks like.

I can tell you now that the decisions I regret the most in my career were the ones I never made: not cutting loose the people who sucked the energy out of the room.

As I sit here in retirement and reflect on my many victories and championships, they all seem so irrelevant. Nobody talks about them, and nobody seems to care. All everyone seems to remember are the good times, the fun we had, and the friends we made. This offers a valuable perspective on the synergy between fun, great leadership, and great performance.

Key takeaways

- Get out in the non-business world, and gain perspective.
- Value attitude over skill every time.
- Don't allow the allure of victory and rewards to compromise your values (it's hard).

LESSON 13

Create an environment where you can shine

Be careful the environment you choose for it will shape you; be careful the friends you choose for you will become like them.

W. Clement Stone

I never really believed that I had the stuff that would allow me to rise to a higher level in the corporate world. I was convinced that my limitations—substandard reading, writing, and math skills and a below-average IQ—made this level of success unattainable. The people I saw in higher positions were so polished and intelligent; they seemed superior to me in every way. I truly didn't think I stood a chance.

As I began to understand my strengths, the power of friendship, and the wonders of teamwork, I realized that the best of me came alive when I was in a trusting environment and surrounded by the right kind of people. I came to know that my style of management worked, my employees were happy, and we continually seemed to outperform teams managed by what I had previously perceived as 'model executives.'

As time passed, my perception of these executives changed. The attitudes that once made them seem polished now revealed the inconsistency between their words and actions. While I once marveled at their intelligence, now I saw their blindness to the simple solutions that lay in front of them. Ultimately, it became clear that the self-confidence I had once admired had robbed them of humility, and their self-reliance had cheated them out of experiencing the true power of teamwork.

There is no doubt that my work experiences and coaching played a big part in my development. Yet, they were not enough to fully explain how my stubbornness, ego, and bravado morphed into a more balanced and practical form of confidence.

As I searched for answers, it became clear that the key to my evolving mindset was the influence of my friends, who accepted me for who I was, didn't devalue me because of my quirkiness and outrageousness, and even loved me more because of it.

There is one particular event that illustrates the impact of personal connections on my growth and development.

Making what you have work for you

The East Coast Celebrity Golf Classic was held in Digby, Nova Scotia, for three days every July. When the tournament was in full swing, the small town came alive with the addition of 250 golfers, 50 celebrities, and countless volunteers. I have had the pleasure to meet and golf with many celebrities, including several Hockey Hall of Famers, Stanley Cup winners, Grammy winners, world champions, and Olympic gold medalists.

The tournament was a three-day party marathon with all these golfers and celebrities stuck in one small town with nowhere to run, which created the real magic. If the same tournament had been held in a big city, they would have scattered around to various bars, or they'd end up going home.

Everyone stayed at the Digby Pines, an old five-star hotel. The tournament took over the hotel and several attached cottages. My friends and I always had a cottage front and center, and that is where the real magic happened.

Before and after golf, we'd gather on our deck, always lucky enough to be joined by some of the biggest names in the Canadian entertainment industry. There, I'd sing along with these world-renowned entertainers while sharing a beer or two with the who's who of the Canadian sports world. I often had to pinch myself to confirm it was real.

Over the years, I got to know some of the celebrities pretty well. I often discussed with them the challenges and obstacles they had to overcome to reach their level of success. These exchanges showed me that these highly accomplished people were dealing with their own issues and limitations, just like me. They simply refused to allow their shit to derail their goals.

I then realized that success was not about having it all but about making what you have work for you. Perhaps if I focused on my strengths instead of being mentally bound by my limitations, I could take the next step on my journey.

There is no doubt that my thirst for a good time pushed me toward a certain type of character, while at the same time, my personal history and life's ups and downs prompted me to search out people I could trust: my wingmen.

Wingman #1 – The cool, confident redneck

One of the regulars at the Digby tournament was Doug Smith, who was also one of the traumatized sailors from our ill-fated boat trip. Doug was a top-notch partier, always on the lookout for a good time. He made friends everywhere he went. You could airdrop him into a remote Japanese village, and he'd be on a first-name basis around town within an hour. Needless to say, he was a must.

Doug had a certain charm about him. He was always quick to pick up a guitar and sing a song while he pounded down a few double rum and Cokes, stopping only to make fun of something or someone.

Having Doug there, along with Johnny Mac and Dan, who were also regulars, was important to me. They were the frontmen; they made the introductions and got the party started, allowing me to easily fold into the fun.

Their presence gave me a sense of comfort. Being surrounded by people I trusted and who accepted me was so empowering! It allowed me to relax, push aside my anxiety, and just let it all hang out.

This feeling was a game-changer. Over time, I came to realize that when I was relaxed and comfortable in my environment, my mental functions improved, my anxiety faded away, my brain fog lifted, and I became unburdened by the mental obstacles that often held me back. I essentially became sharper, smarter, and more confident! At the center of this transformation were these friends who accepted me for being me.

Doug was quite a character. He would have his Digby stumbles over the years, rolling golf carts and sliding down a twenty-foot embankment, falling off a ten-foot deck onto his face. Hell, he suffered more cuts and bruises than our one-time golfing partner and Hockey Hall of Famer, goaltender Gump Worsley, on a Saturday night at the Maple Leafs Gardens.

Doug's misadventures in Digby had him almost elevated to celebrity status, not because he survived the rolls or the falls (well, maybe a little) but because of how he reacted, so cool and confident. He used to say to everyone, "What's the big deal? Just having a little fun!" He owned it, and people loved him because of it. There was something to be learned here: own who you are, mistakes, stumbles, and all. God knows, if I was going to have any success at all, I would have to do that.

Doug is a successful financial planner, stubborn and opinionated, a Trump-supporting, anti-government, anti-COVID type of guy, yet trustworthy and loyal to a fault.

On one occasion, on his way to my place in Costa Rica, security noticed something odd in his carry-on bag, which turned out to be a box of bullets...

Doug had brought his hunting bag and apparently forgot to check it for bullets, which he explained to the security agents. Oddly enough, they accepted his story, and he told them to "throw them in the garbage," to which they replied that they could not do it without getting the police involved. As a brilliant alternative, they suggested that he put them in his checked luggage and send them through to Costa Rica. Having no choice, he agreed. Absolutely bonkers!

Doug got on the plane to Costa Rica, had a slew of drinks, and landed in San Jose. When he went through Immigration, they discovered that he had only four weeks left on his passport; you needed three months minimum to enter. As a result, they denied him entry and put him on the next flight back to Canada. While he waited, they locked him in a secure room overnight with an armed guard keeping watch, and yes, he still had twenty live rounds rattling around in his suitcase.

Knowing that explaining the bullets to the Costa Rican police in a foreign language while intoxicated might not go so well, he hatched a plan to dispose of his contraband. When they finally let him go to the washroom, he snuck the bullets into his small travel bag and covertly slid the bullets into the garbage. Lucky or stupid, it was a tossup; nonetheless, the headline "Drunken Canadian Terrorist attack on Costa Rica thwarted by authorities" never made it to the news networks. So, we'll call it a victory.

The next morning, they sent him home. Doug, undeterred, went directly to the passport office, told them what happened (minus the bullets), and in thirty-six hours, he was back in Costa Rica with a new passport and one hell of a story.

What a guy! Setting aside the stupidity of the bullets, the outdated passport fiasco, and the near-international incident, his resilience and commitment to get his ass back to Costa Rica was legendary.

Wingman #2 – The likable mad scientist

Another character who really elevated my thinking was Rod Savoie. I first laid eyes on Rod at our first competitive Ringette meeting. He was sitting at the back of the room, unshaven, in a black leather jacket; he looked like a hitman.

It was not until our first tournament that Monique met Rod and realized she knew him from high school. I said to her, "That's the guy I told you about. Is he going to be trouble?"

"Yep," she replied with a big laugh.

Rod would become my partner in crime for many years. He was a regular at my parties, including the night the 'Noise Nazi' first reared her pretty head (it was his fault). I soon learned that Rod is nothing like he looks. He has a Ph.D. in engineering with a specialization in fluid dynamics (whatever that means) and is undoubtedly one of the most intelligent guys I know.

We shared many memorable experiences as the Ringette world took us to points far and wide. Wherever we went, Rod used his outgoing style to befriend pretty much everyone he met. His likability factor was off the charts, and I learned to appreciate it, which led me to invite him to many of my business-related social events, where his outgoing personality took the spotlight off me, allowing me to relax and be at my best.

I used the same rationale when I invited people to Digby. I knew the celebrities didn't come to our deck to see me; hell no, it was Rod,

Doug, and the other hoodlums I brought along that had them lining up. I knew my limitations; I was under no illusion about my (lack of) charismatic appeal and knew very well that I needed strong wingmen around me to fill in my gaps.

My strategy of bringing friends to company events was often seen by my fellow executives as an abuse of company funds. I saw it differently; my job was to build relationships and get the most out of customer interactions, and my strategy achieved exactly that. So, I ignored the naysayers and did what I thought was best.

On Rod's first morning in Digby, he was driving the golf cart with a hockey star in the passenger seat. Rod decided to take a shortcut through a field, which was covered in high grass. Suddenly, the cart fell hard into a hidden ditch, sending our celebrity guest flying through the windshield. The poor guy took the windshield with him as he rolled onto the grass.

Rod's initial thought was, *I've killed him.* Thankfully, he was okay but extremely pissed off. Rod apologized frantically, helped him to his feet, and in unique Rod-style, hugged him, handed him a beer, and off they went like nothing ever happened.

Rod's personality is an interesting one. He is a man of extremes, loud and outspoken, yet sensitive and self-reflective. He is intelligent but has common sense (well, most of the time). He is focused on himself but, at the same time, extremely giving, and while he displays great self-confidence, he is plagued with anxiety.

As you can imagine, these contrasting forces have caused him to run amok more than a few times. Once, he was in France with Caroline, his Ringette-playing daughter, who had become an accomplished singer-songwriter and was performing at a festival. One night, Rod went out with his daughter and her music friends. Of course, Rod did what came naturally; he was the life of the party, crushing drinks like it was Mardi Gras. The next morning, Caroline asked him, "Who's the parent here?" She told him to start acting like a responsible adult. He heard her loud and clear, and I'm sure it bothered him to no end.

The following day, he decided, "I'm only drinking water; I'll show her!" Well, Rod being Rod, he drank so much water that he had to be hospitalized for overhydration (also called hyponatremia or water intoxication). It was bizarre, considering all the booze he had consumed over the years. Unbelievable, but pure Rod!

He's quite a cat, a successful mad-scientist type. A true intellect, capable of discussing concepts from the 1s and 0s of computer programming to the origins of the universe, he also has this common-sense, street-smart acumen that allows him to relate to the people around him. It is truly a combination I have rarely seen.

Hanging with Rod gave me a certain confidence. Being able to hold my own (and then some) with him on most subjects during our countless debates gave me the feeling that I could handle anyone, anywhere, at any level.

Wingman #3 – ADHD... on steroids

Then there was Scott, one of those 'you'd have to see it to believe it' characters. The man is a walking contradiction, an angel sent from hell. Fiercely intelligent, strategic, loveable, and caring, yet the most sporadic, free-spirited trouble magnet you'd ever meet.

One day, I was sitting in the parking lot in Terra Nova National Park in Newfoundland, taking off my golf shoes, when this guy started talking to me like he had known me for twenty-five years. He had this great big smile on his face, and he talked a mile a minute while laughing at everything he said. I thought, "This is one happy dude." That was my introduction to Scott Cole.

Scott was the national director for one of the generic drug companies, and although this was our first personal encounter, his company did a considerable amount of business with us in Atlantic Canada.

A few weeks later, Guy and I received a message from Scott inviting us to a golf school on Prince Edward Island, which we gladly accepted. On the first evening, Scott's company held a reception. That was the night we got to know one another. At some point, I noticed that Scott and his friend Gordie Lebel kept disappearing throughout the evening.

As a seasoned grass smoker myself, my stoner senses tingled. I knew exactly what they were up to: They were off sneaking a puff somewhere.

I tracked them down in Scott's room, where I banged on the door, yelling, "I know you're in there, and I know what you're doing." All I could hear from the other side of the door was laughter. "Are you a cop?" I heard. "Hell no," I replied. "Let me in." They did, and we smoked a big joint. No better way to bond.

This marked the beginning of a friendship and a business relationship with Scott that would span decades. When it came to business, it was serious, which we both took as a challenge while trying to get the best deal out of the other. In the end, we would both walk away thinking we had outsmarted the other fellow.

Scott had this big smile and oozed personality. He could talk to anyone, CEO or truck driver, with genuine interest. Status made no difference to him. His approach was a marvel to watch. His confidence and enthusiasm were contagious. And his thirst for a good time set us off on a few adventures, including fishing excursions in northern British Columbia and the Gander River in Newfoundland as well as trips to the Caribbean and our favorite place, Costa Rica.

On our first trip to Costa Rica, I was introduced to Scott's driving skills, which led to many near-death experiences as he haphazardly navigated through the narrow, windy mountain roads at twice the speed limit with music blaring. He usually had a smoke in one hand, a beer in the other, and he would try to make eye contact with the person in the back seat while passing a car on a narrow mountain road. The sad part was that he thought he was a great driver. I am sure he can parallel park like nobody's business, but his recklessness and lack of attention made driving with him a nightmare.

On a trip to the Osa Peninsula in southern Costa Rica, the couple who had traveled there with us had to ride back with Scott. When they returned home, I asked, "How was Scott's driving?"

"Really good. He's a fantastic driver."

"Then why is the car's fender lying at your feet?"

"Oh, that." Then, they started laughing uncontrollably, realizing that Scott had convinced them that the loss of the fender wasn't his fault and that he was indeed a "super good driver."

That was Scott. He lived life like he drove, running in all directions at the same time. He could convince anyone of anything, and he was always able to rationalize his actions and justify his perspective.

He was exciting and exhausting to hang with; you just never knew what was around the corner. We even ended up buying a house together in Costa Rica. This is something that we, the Brennans, would have never done on our own, but it allowed us to experience people, places, and things that we wouldn't have had the opportunity to experience otherwise. Every aspect of that new adventure broadened my perspective and expanded my comfort zone.

Choose your friends wisely

Scott, Doug, and Rod were all 'superstar' characters. They all possessed a profound ability to connect with people and a world-be-damned attitude balanced by practical wisdom. They had no façade. They weren't trying to be cool or create an illusion of being something they were not; they simply were!

As I reflected on my connections with them, I came to the realization that these three guys were no different from most of the friends I was typically drawn to. Tom, John Van from STU, Joanne, Rob, Dan, Johnny Mac, Lennie, Joanne, and now Rod, Scott, and Doug were all different but undoubtedly cut from the same cloth. The experiences we shared were invaluable to me. Their tolerance, patience, and acceptance of me seemed to stabilize me.

If I had surrounded myself with two-faced people—people prepared to stay silent as I ran amok and who would put their own agendas before friendship and loyalty—I might have never learned the lesson I needed to become the person I am today.

Feeling accepted, valued, and challenged made all the difference. Science seems to back up my empirical observations. Researchers have concluded that "friendships are an important source of happiness, well-being, physical health, and longevity" and often link the quality of one's friendships to life satisfaction.[5]

I couldn't agree more. If there is one lesson I learned from all the good that came from my many connections with very special humans, it is that few choices will have a bigger impact on your life than your choice of friends.

Am I a leader?

As I went through my middle management years, I asked myself if I was getting any closer to becoming that elusive creature called a leader. My successes and high level of team engagement suggested that I was on the right track.

Yet, I didn't get the feeling that I was what the higher-ups were looking for. Yeah, they kept telling me I had potential, but I never got invited to any of the leadership retreats. The way I talked and interacted with the employees and customers was often criticized by HR and other executives as being inappropriate, not executive-like, and too rough around the edges.

Still, it felt right to me. I was having fun, my teams were motivated and engaged, customers were happy, and we kept hitting our numbers out of the park.

I was happy to be in my little corner of the world, far away from corporate interference. I undoubtedly matured over the years, and the support and tolerance of my friends allowed me the time to figure out who the hell I was.

I learned that when I was comfortable and trusted my environment, my worries and inhibitions fell to the side, my anxiety disappeared, and I became the best version of myself. The countless lessons in humility tempered my stubbornness and softened my ego, allowing me to consider other points of view and even (sometimes) admit that I was wrong.

My formal psychological assessment helped me understand how my brain worked and how to maximize what I had, which I achieved by becoming a master of organization, delegation, simplicity, and clarity.

I made it a point to search for people with the skills and perspective I lacked. Each team member became a critical piece to the puzzle, and when I was lucky enough to get all the right pieces in the right places and in just the right environment, it was pure magic.

But let me tell you, it was never easy. Outside forces and misleading narratives were constantly trying to push us off course. The pressure to conform, the weight of needless complexity, and the misplaced executive ego, coupled with executive unawareness, made it almost impossible to stay on task.

To counterbalance those realities, I spent most of my time removing obstacles and deflecting interference in trying to give my team enough runway to get the job done. As I moved into my executive role at McKesson, I would cling tightly to my way of doing things, knowing it would be the key to my success and even my workplace survival.

That said, I was under no delusions, and I knew I'd have to adjust to a new company and culture, learn to compromise more, lose my 'party boy' image, continue to mask my limitations, and at times, even accept and support decisions I disagreed with. This was not an enticing prospect for the likes of me. Nevertheless, I was excited about the new challenges ahead and ready to bob and weave my way around what I didn't know and find help when I needed it. If I was gonna make it, I knew it would be with more than 'a little help from my friends.'

Key takeaways

- The people who will positively influence you will come in all shapes, sizes, and personalities.
- Create an environment where you can shine.

LESSON 14

Make everyone accountable, including you!

Culture does not change because we desire to change it. . . the culture reflects the realities of people working together every day

Frances Hesselbein

In the next chapter of my life, I would have power over a lot of people, and I would learn how to empower them. I would also learn a few things about the 'us vs. them' mentality that dominated many aspects of business. I was not a fan; I would fight against it for years. Ultimately, I would master the art of building successful teams and embrace my singularity. Rather than imitating the executives I had met in the past, I tried to find my own way to do things, and to my astonishment, it worked!

Getting rid of 'us vs. them'

As the summer of 2000 rolled in, I was excited to start my new career, taking the lead role at McKesson in Atlantic Canada. I knew the company well from having worked with them throughout my years at Shoppers. Yet, as I entered the business, I was shocked at how strained the relationship was between management and the staff. I remember my first walk through the Halifax warehouse. No one spoke, and people refused to even look in my direction. Frankly, it was pretty intimidating!

The office itself was a highly regimented work environment. Everyone knew their place and did exactly what they were told. Many of the management groups operated using this "us vs. them" mentality. They believed that the only way to get things done was through total obedience to an exorbitant number of rules. They believed that distribution was a rough and tough business and that holding employees' feet to the fire was essential to getting the job done.

After a few months of coming to understand the people and the operation, I jumped in with both feet, taking my plan to the team. I told them, "If you have concerns, that's fine, but speak up now because when we conclude these discussions, there will be only one path forward. There'll be no second-guessing, no water-cooler talk. So, speak your mind and express your point of view, or I'll interpret your silence as full agreement."

The result was many no-holds-barred conversations and a lot of me explaining what I was trying to accomplish and how. We started making changes in the Halifax office: eliminating complexity, simplifying processes, reassessing job expectations, and clarifying each employee's accountabilities. Then, we loosened the rules to let people use their brainpower.

The employees' initial reaction was positive, followed by skepticism. They wondered if they were being set up. But when they realized we weren't messing around, they relaxed and got to work like never before.

In the warehouse, it was clear that the poor relationships and low productivity were due to a cold, hard application of the rules, which were made without feeling or common sense. The manager at the time was unwilling or unable to operate within our new operating philosophy, so I unapologetically cut him loose.

When the new manager came on board, we took note of the employees' issues and concerns. We fixed what we could and explained why we couldn't fix what was beyond our means, but mostly we listened. After some time, and as a direct result of our new engagement approach—really, after they realized we weren't full of shit—attitudes started to change.

You could feel the change in the air. I was even able to walk through the warehouse without fear of being run over by a forklift! As the months went by, employees across the business started to see the benefits of the new way of doing things. This had a major positive impact on morale, highlighted by the ease with which a new union contract was negotiated in just a couple of weeks. In the past, this type of negotiation had typically taken more than a year. We later instituted the same changes in Newfoundland, resulting in their contract taking only two days to finalize, which was unheard of.

Our broader engagement strategy didn't end there. I was fixated on creating an environment where employees could enjoy their workplace, speak freely, and give their opinions without fear of reprisal. In the past, there was a Christmas party and service awards, but it was all boring and devoid of meaning. It was just your typical check-the-box, HR-directive type of thing. I convinced my management group that we needed to spice things up, starting with the service awards. We needed to make them more personal and heartfelt. The bottom line was, "Can you act like you frigging care?" Oh, how they struggled with the idea at first. Nonetheless, I took the bull by the horns, and the employees loved it, particularly the warehouse staff. I once heard them mutter after a few beers, "Maybe management aren't such assholes after all."

The combination of these rejigged events and the new positive workplace caused employees to change, laugh, and excel at their jobs. They even started to see the humor in situations that would have pissed them off in the past. While we were implementing all these changes, the management group was still trying to figure out this uncompromising and often aggressive new boss who was also not lacking in sense of humor and approachability.

On one occasion, Customer Service Manager Winnie and Accounts Receivables Manager Kathy were dealing with an issue with a customer, and they asked me for advice. I told them what to do, and they tried to solve the problem my way, with no success. They then came back to me to look for a different solution.

Stubborn as I am, I told them, "You have the solution and, frankly, I don't care if the Pope calls. That's my final decision." Quickly, it became glaringly obvious that 'my way' sucked. I later had some real shame-faced apologizing to do. I ate a nice piece of humble pie with plenty of 'I told you so's' to wash it down.

Two days later, Winnie, Kathy, and half of the staff showed up at my office chanting in unison, "Rick, the Pope called," and presented me with a Pope's hat made of cardboard. Truth be told, it was more like a dunce hat.

This was just one more in a long list of lessons in humility. More importantly, it showed me that we had arrived as a team. The fact that my subordinates were comfortable enough to make fun of the boss for his pigheadedness was a true sign that we had come together.

Aside from all the fun and giggles, our division had become a well-oiled machine; employees were accountable, performance mattered, and reaching our collective goals was paramount.

A dog with a bone!

It was during this period that I introduced the theme of a 'dog with a bone' to illustrate to the group our total commitment to reaching our goals without compromise and to get their head around my motto, "No more excuses; just make it happen!"

We did have one small incident when Winnie told her Customer Service group, "We're like a dog with a bon*ER*." Not quite, but close enough! Of course, we didn't throw people to the wolves expecting them to jump every hurdle on their own. We set up a system of support, dealt with unforeseen issues and obstacles as a group, and readjusted our game plan when required. Yet, everyone was accountable for their performance, and they knew it.

What most executives found surprising was that my team had no problem accepting this high level of accountability. Their goals were clear and fair, everyone was treated equally, the process was simple, and if the unexpected happened, we were there to support and figure it out together. People felt good that what they did mattered and were proud that their actions were essential to the team's success.

Unconventional chemistry

Creating team chemistry was at the core of my strategy. I knew that in order to be successful, I needed a motivated and hardworking team around me. One of the things I did to keep my teams connected and motivated was facilitating regular out-of-the-office events. Because I was a bit of a hard-ass, I found that getting out of the office and having a little fun, which I was good at, could balance things off nicely. These events also allowed the team to get to know the other side of Rick—the funny, animated, and socially relaxed guy that I was.

During one of our Eastern Canada management meetings, Sheldon Bowman, our sales manager, was 'volun-told' to take the lead in one of our team-building activities. To commemorate his participation, he wrote a piece that I think illustrates the type of fun we had:

A Rita surprise

During an Eastern Canadian marketplace meeting, Rick decided to surprise our Quebec colleagues with some 'good ole' maritime hospitality.

My assignment was to imitate Rita MacNeil, a legendary singer from Cape Breton, and sing one of her greatest hits, Working Man. I recruited a few of our fellow maritime executives to stand in as her renowned backup band, The Men of the Deeps. I figured if I was going to look stupid, so should they!

Truth be told, I can't sing worth a lick, but Rick has a way of making things look like fun and can talk you into doing things you never thought you'd do. Fucker!

So, I guzzled down a few beers and got primed for my involuntary debut.

I was in the back room getting ready, stripped down to my underpants, stuffing my bra with tissue, when I looked up to find a group of Japanese tourists peering through the window, watching my transformation. I'll never forget the look of horror in their eyes as they gasped for air.

Oh, well, welcome to Cape Breton!

Rick had told the group that we had hired the 'real' Rita MacNeil, so they were pumped up for the big show. As I entered the room in my long dress, large black hat, and bare feet (Rita's signature look), people looked at me with a certain kind of oddness. I even heard someone say, "Man, Rita looks bad. Is she sick?" But they quickly recognized me and were soon rolling in the aisles with laughter.

I was quite the sight. We even managed to get the VPs for Eastern Canada to join The Men of the Deeps and cover their faces in coal dust. Oh, what a time we had!

While this type of foolishness was normal for the Atlantic group, the Montreal crowd had never really experienced anything like this before. Yet, they joined in, and we all had a great night.

During those few days, we also went sailing on the Bras d'Or Lakes, had a few late-night bonfires on the beach, ate lots of lobster, and drank a large amount of alcohol. The event was a great team builder and allowed the two groups to get to know each other.

Although we knew each of our Quebec counterparts in a boardroom setting, this nontraditional approach cemented our relationships and changed our dynamic, paving the way for a different level of cooperation.

Just a great example of how getting out of the box and having a little fun can help to build long-lasting relationships.

Rita MacNeil (aka Sheldon Bowman)

Our fun was not restricted to out-of-office events. The atmosphere at the office was pleasant. There was a lot of joking around, and laughing was commonplace. Dick Peterson, who ran the Moncton facility, was a commonsense, straightforward guy. He wasn't shy about expressing his opinion or even playing a joke on me. Don't take my word for it; you can hear it from the horse's mouth:

A real shocker

I am sure that some great business guru has written that to impress your new boss, you must first get to know them and their management style. Once you understand the aforementioned style, you are supposed to conduct yourself accordingly.

My problem with following this advice was twofold: first, my new boss was Rick Brennan, and second, I wasn't sure he had any style—aforementioned or otherwise.

Therefore, I thought I'd try a different approach and opted for the more unconventional shock therapy route. I had recently obtained a fake click-type pen that contained a battery and a nasty shocker. What I did know about Rick was that he was nobody's fool. Waltzing in there and handing him a pen wasn't going to work. I was going to have to engage him in a competition of some sort, a challenge, something to pique his interest.

At this time, Rick worked out of our old boardroom. He had just moved into the Moncton location from Halifax, and we didn't have a proper office for him. Heck, if my little trick was to go bad for me, he may very well find that a new office had just become available.

The boardroom was average length but narrow across. Rick's rather large desk was up against the side wall with just enough space to walk around it to get to his chair. The chair itself wasn't much more than two feet off the back wall. The whole setup looked cramped and confined. What I did like about it was that I figured I could escape the room long before he could get out from behind the desk and grab me.

I worked out the challenge as follows: Rick could pick any number between 1 and 10, and I would tell him what it was on the first guess. Now, here was the rub: I told him I didn't trust him, and even if I guessed the number, he might just say, "No, it wasn't that." So, to make it appear like an afterthought, I said, "You better write it down. That way, there is no changing the answer once I guess it."

The trap was sprung, and the bait was set. A smile flashed across his face as he started to think hard about what hard-to-guess number he could write down. I smiled too, but I wasn't thinking about any numbers.

At this point, only a second or two had elapsed, but it was still enough time for me to imagine my whole professional career passing before my eyes. Had I lost my mind? What was I thinking? Was it too late to reach out and snatch the pen from his hand? It was.

The second he pushed down on the silver clicker on top of that pen, I heard him scream. Then, he tried as hard as he could to extricate himself from his chair. He must have thought his office chair had become electrified and was trying to kill him.

The problem with trying to remove himself from the chair, which he believed was trying to kill him, was that it was so close to the wall that there just wasn't enough room to manoeuver. The excruciating pain he was feeling didn't make things any easier for Rick.

First, his knee came up at lightning speed, and this would have been helpful in this situation if it had not crashed violently into the drawer under his desk. Next, the chair, which was firing backward at the speed of an ejector seat, crashed into the wall directly behind him.

Finally, the pen itself was hurled straight up at the ceiling and bounced off. This entire sequence of events took less than three seconds to unfold.

Any thoughts of self-preservation I had were out the window. Never mind that Rick's makeshift office did not have a window. First off, I failed to control a fit of laughter, the kind one can only truly enjoy while watching someone else in peril. It's as primitive and simple as the man who slips on a banana peel—the joke just never gets old. So long as it is not you doing the slipping.

The first words out of Rick's mouth were, "Oh, my God! That's great! You have to bring that pen to Digby." I kid you not. Far from being upset, he was excited about playing that kind of joke during our annual golf tournament.

I think that illustrates Rick's management style. I guess you can say he loves a good joke, even if he is the butt of it. This may not be the kind of management style you can find in books written by business gurus, but it is the kind I like.

(Dick Peterson)

Dick's trick, Sheldon's willingness to be the butt of everyone's jokes, the presentation of the Pope's hat, and so many other planned and unplanned events were truly at the core of our special team chemistry.

Many would argue that business shouldn't be about fun but about performance. I totally agree. To the naysayers out there: Our results were pretty astonishing over the next number of years. Atlantic Canada led the country in almost every operational measurement: productivity, employee and customer engagement scores, error rates, and on-time deliveries. Meanwhile, sales and financial results were always well above target.

Yet, that was still only half of the story. We had customers to deal with. Our independent-banner customers were a fickle crowd. Having their business was one thing; keeping it was quite another. As a result, we attended countless meetings, social gatherings, and conferences in an attempt to solidify our relationships with both the office staff and store management teams.

I was always lucky enough to attend the yearly Pharmachoice Pharmacy groups' congress. It was usually held somewhere warm, and I always brought my wife and the kids. I came to appreciate the power of family connections. Having all of our spouses and kids building relationships among themselves had a certain power of its own. The depth of these relationships would be key to ensuring that McKesson kept its business.

Relationships save the day

Pharmachoice was about one year from contract renewal when, under the cloak of darkness, their board agreed to a deal with our competitor and to leave McKesson. The terms of their new deal were finalized, including an agreement to build a new warehouse in St. John's, Newfoundland, for the benefit of a few owners.

With the formal agreement completed, the board only had to get the membership's approval at the upcoming general meeting, which I'm sure they saw as a mere formality. The general meeting was only a few weeks away; if we had any chance of influencing the membership, we needed to jump into action.

After a quick discussion with our executive office and a consultation with a few of our key contacts at Pharmachoice, Sheldon and I jumped into separate cars and started visiting owners, who turned out to be unaware of the board's intentions. We pushed the store owners, one by one, to reject the board's plan. We were definitely like a 'dog with a bon*ER*!' It seems Winnie may have been right after all!

At the general meeting, the membership voted down the board's proposal and forced them to renegotiate a deal with McKesson. Yes, we'd won the battle and kept the business, but to seal the deal, we'd have to give them a market-leading deal, which made total sense at that time in our growth cycle. Keeping Pharmachoice's business was critical to us and devastating to our competitor, forcing their closure only a few years later.

What a victory! Nobody thought we could pull it off! No one understood the depth of our relationships and how much customers valued the quality of our service.

On the flip side—there's always a flip side—Sheldon and I were promised major bonuses if we could turn the Pharmachoice decision around, but when it came time to pay, management reneged on the payments. This was not typical of McKesson, but it illustrates that a company is just the sum of the people it employs. It wasn't McKesson that decided not to pay. It wasn't a corporate decision; there were no boardroom meetings. The Senior Vice President (SVP) at the time simply decided not to honor the agreement. Although the monetary outcome was an eye-opening disappointment, I quickly moved on. It wouldn't change my life.

I had many experiences during those early years. I was lucky to be hundreds of miles away from the influence of the corporate establishment. Unlike other regional managers, I had direct responsibility for both sales and operations, which allowed our unit to have one single, consolidated plan of attack.

During those first few years at McKesson, I was constantly drawing on my coaching experiences and my days at Shoppers. More than anything, I was committed to being me, using the skills that came naturally, and embracing what made me different rather than conforming to who others thought I should be.

I relied on a simple plan, a straightforward dialogue, and clear expectations to get people to understand what I wanted them to do. I would come to understand that no matter what a wonderful, smart, and charming leader you may think you are, people can't follow what they don't understand, and they can't run when bound by rules.

Accountability was the foundation of both our operational and employee engagement success. It was applied fairly and consistently, which ensured equity among employees and allowed for a more relaxed atmosphere.

The idea of having a high level of accountability seems to confuse and scare most managers. They interpret accountability as a negative activity that reduces flexibility and stifles empowerment. This couldn't be further from the truth. Knowing what's expected of you—when, where, and how to do your job—is what every employee hopes for. Flexibility and empowerment reside within this framework. Clear, simple, understandable, and fair expectations are the foundations of strong employee engagement.

Key takeaways

- Be aggressive in action and attitude.
- Accountability and fairness are at the core of employee engagement.
- Find the humor in difficult situations.

LESSON 15

Look for what others don't see

Any fool can know; the point is to understand.

Albert Einstein

Throughout my career, simplicity, clarity, organization, reliance on people, and a dogmatic approach to achieving my goals were the cornerstones of my management style. My style worked for me. My teams were motivated, they operated efficiently, and our performance and financial measurements were usually top-tier.

Rarely did we waste time putting out fires or dealing with complaints that plagued other regions. Instead, we focused our time and energy on helping our customers grow their businesses. I like to think that we were more of a partner than a supplier.

There was nothing fancy about our approach, and maybe it was even a little boring. It often caused executives from outside our region to remark, "How lucky you are to have customers and unions that are so easy to deal with." We just laughed and shook our heads at their total lack of awareness. They truly had no idea how hard our team worked and how many hours were invested in building those 'easy' relationships!

Dodge complexity at every turn

As I climbed the ladder, this 'executive unawareness' only seemed to be more prevalent. There was an inherent belief that a vast amount of data, analysis, and human capital was what was required for any project to be successful. It was complexity over simplicity, with people typically discarding the obvious and simple solution, often with a touch of arrogance. It was almost as if complexity validated their existence. Things apparently had to be difficult to have value.

Despite this prevailing complexity mindset, my team and I would hide away in our little corner of the world, hundreds of miles from the national office, quietly focused on making things as simple as possible. We had experienced great success over the last number of years, having secured one hundred percent of the available business and the highest performance numbers in the country.

Yet, this success was becoming our burden. We knew that memories were short in the corporate world, and we had to find a way to grow, or we could soon go from star of the show to loser in the crowd—and fast. Worse, the bosses might start spending their time at our office trying to fix what wasn't broken, and they'd soon have us drowning in a world of complexity. God, anything but that!

There is always room to grow

As we (the Atlantic team) pondered our 'success dilemma,' it became clear that our plan would have to be big and bold if we hoped to reset our growth protection. We regretfully agreed that we had to restructure the region, potentially closing our Moncton and Halifax facilities and replacing them with a new state-of-the-art building in Moncton.

Aside from that, we had to deal with our sales issue. What do you do when you have all the available business? The answer was surprisingly simple: We'd have to get some of the unavailable business. This would be no easy task; it would require another company to agree to restructure their business and lay off their employees.

Creating opportunity

We looked at our options and thought our best chances lay with Sobeys and Lawtons Pharmacy, which had an aging warehouse and a business model that might benefit from our infrastructure. This is where our two projects intersected; one of the partners in the construction group we thought might be a good fit was Johnny Mac's brother, Gerard, whom I had gotten to know well over the years.

Gerard had strong ties in the Sobeys world, and the construction company he was now involved with was building several projects for them. I planned to leverage his relationships to help build a few connections of my own. The biggest challenge I faced was the ingrained distrust that many on the Sobeys management team had for McKesson. In fact, some of them had previously been fired from McKesson.

The first thing I did to try to remedy the situation was to send out key members of my team to meet and offer an olive branch to the McKesson haters. My gesture was relatively successful. I also enlisted guys like Scott Cole, Johnny Mac, and Dan White, who had solid relationships with the Sobeys team, to reinforce the high level of trust and confidence they had for me and my team. As a result of this feel-good campaign, we managed to get them to agree to sit down and have a discussion, and lo and behold, we quickly found potential opportunities.

Yet, I could still feel the awkwardness around the table. I just knew that the resentment was still burning hot with many of the Sobeys people. I thought that maybe some sort of outing with spouses would allow everyone to get to know each other on a personal level. I enlisted Gerard's help, and we got the group to agree to attend a U2 concert on the hill in Moncton and stay at my cottage for the weekend.

The weekend, the Friday pre-night party and sing-along, the concert, the bus trip to and from—all of it was an absolute blast, and it had the desired effect. With everyone feeling more relaxed and the sins of our predecessors buried and put to rest, we got down to business.

While this was going on, we were still in the process of planning the construction of the new Moncton building, and the national office gave us clear instructions to involve McKesson's corporate Real Estate group out of San Francisco, who were responsible for all construction for McKesson worldwide.

The instant the Real Estate group arrived, we were shocked by their arrogance and lack of interest in our regional agenda. Not being someone to roll over without a good reason, I charged ahead, probably more recklessly than I should have. My attitude was 'screw them,' and I just kept pushing and pushing, getting myself in and out of hot water for several months.

In the end, with support from Nick, my boss, MRE finally folded, and construction began. As we announced to the staff that we would be closing the building in Halifax, I was warned by our national office that the union would undoubtedly cause trouble through the transition.

Over the next few months, we started talking to the staff and union representatives, explaining our rationale for closing the building. Though they weren't happy about losing their jobs, they understood and accepted our logic. The result of these negotiations was astonishing; employees worked incredibly hard until the final box was shipped.

I was so proud of them. This experience confirmed my belief that honest communication and solid relationships built over time can neutralize many of the negative aspects of business. After a few ups and downs, construction was completed, and the transition from the old building to the new one was seamless.

Watch out for the curve

All along, we had been negotiating with Sobeys, and after much back and forth, we were at the last stages of finalizing an agreement. That's when McKesson announced the purchase of Drug Trading, which included the retail pharmacy assets of Guardian, the Independent Drug Association (IDA), and Medicine Shoppe.

Sobeys instantly killed the deal. In the minds of the Sobeys executives, the moment McKesson went into retail, we became a competitor, and Sobeys had a clear policy about not doing business with competitors.

What a disappointment after all that work! It all went down the drain over something that was entirely beyond our control. Then, as if that wasn't devastating enough to our sales plan, Pharmasave National announced they were leaving McKesson for a competitor, a major blow to McKesson nationally and potentially to my group in short order.

A few years earlier, Johnny Mac had become president of Pharmasave Atlantic, and he and I had negotiated a five-year Atlantic Canada Pharmasave/McKesson distribution agreement, which had eighteen months left on it. Hopefully, that would give me the time to convince some stores to jump ship.

During the PharmaChoice board rebellion a few years earlier, I learned a few tricks, and I was confident I could turn the tide in my direction. I sure wasn't going to give up without a fight.

Our reputation, quality of service, and longstanding history with our customers couldn't be matched by our competitors. Pharmasave National's decision had the potential to negatively impact each store's profitability and, more importantly, the owners' incomes. My strategy was clear: Make it all about the dollars and cents.

I was also aware, however, that it was a big deal for stores to leave their present banner, so my job wouldn't be an easy one. I was hoping that if I could get one group of stores to jump ship first, that might be the catalyst I needed to convince other stores to follow suit. It was time to call on some old friends.

By this time, Johnny Mac had left his role as president of Pharmasave Atlantic and had become a store owner. He had just partnered with the McDonough group as they expanded their empire with a major five-store acquisition in Nova Scotia. I was hoping that the strength of my relationship with John and our history of quality of service would convince his group of stores to flip banners. There was a catch: He had partners, and they would have to agree.

Luckily enough, I also had a strong relationship with the McDonough family. I had often socialized with Art McDonough Sr. and Art Jr. over the years, developing a very natural bond with them. If you've gotten this far in the book, you already guessed that if there was bonding, there was also some form of mischief involved.

A-waxing he will go!

On one occasion, Scott Cole, Art McDonough Jr., and I went down to the beautiful island of Aruba in the company of our wives. One night, we all went to supper. At one point in the evening, someone commented, "That plastic wrap can be as strong as steel. If you wrapped someone tightly enough, they'd never escape." I immediately reacted, "Bullshit!" Then someone jokingly suggested, "Let's wrap Rick around a palm tree!"

Scott talked to the waiter, who returned in a matter of minutes with an industrial-sized roll of plastic wrap. I was overwhelmingly against the idea, but the group persisted and wore me down. So, I declared, "Okay, I'll let you wrap me, but if I escape, Art has to get his back waxed." Art, who was covered in three-inch-long body hair, reluctantly agreed. Now I was motivated!

In preparation for my 'public wrapping,' I concealed a fork in my pocket just in case my theory was wrong. They found a palm tree, and the wrapping began. As they were going at it, I pushed out my chest and arms, just enough to give me a little flexibility. They must have gone around the tree fifty times, giggling like schoolgirls, so confident in their victory. When they were done, they triumphantly chanted, "Okay, get out of that, shithead." Then, I relaxed my chest and arms, poked a hole in the wrap with my finger, and escaped within seconds! I didn't even need my concealed cutlery.

The next morning (unknown to Art), I went directly to the spa and booked an appointment for his back waxing. I then found him at the beach leisurely enjoying the morning sun and advised him of his appointment. He was shocked that I had followed through (not the typical vendor/customer interaction), but forget that! A deal is a deal, and a-waxing he would go.

I took him by the hand, led him down to the spa, and the deforestation began. I hung around just long enough to hear his screams. Then, I ran back to the beach—laughing all the way—to report that the torture had begun.

We were still chuckling when Art came back with puffy eyes and a back you could see your reflection in. Sadly for him, they had only removed a perfect square of hair from his back, leaving three inches of puffy hair covering his shoulders and arms. He looked like a total idiot. Bonus!

We busted a gut laughing at him. Art's wife Shelley was so embarrassed that she marched him directly back to the torture chamber and got the rest of his overcoat ripped off right. Update: Shelly now makes sure Art gets a regular shearing!

The events of the week created quite a connection between the McDonoughs and the Brennans.

Pushing relationships to the breaking point

On our return, we all got back to trying to finalize a deal. I was able to arrange a pretty aggressive package to pull them over, but then, out of the blue, they were approached by Sobeys to join a new Independent Banner they were hoping to launch. They were offered terms and financial advantages that I just couldn't compete with.

As you can probably appreciate, I was getting a little frustrated with all the curveballs being thrown my way. Yet, this is where my stubbornness and determination became a tremendous asset. I refused to let this deal die and, undeterred, I kept at it, almost pushing our relationship to the breaking point.

Thankfully, I had support from Art Sr., who had been around the block a few times. He challenged his partners to look at our history together—the promises made and broken, the level of trust and respect, the depth of our relationship—and asked them to compare it to the attractive yet untested alternative.

As a result of Art Sr.'s wise words and his partners' belief in our ability to come through in the end, we finalized a deal and flipped their stores to Guardian Pharmacies.

The announcement of their defection from Pharmasave sent shock waves through the market, becoming the catalyst I was hoping for. It caused other Pharmasave stores to reexamine the pros and cons of leaving McKesson Atlantic, resulting in another fifteen high-volume Atlantic stores flipping to Guardian. It was a double victory for McKesson: We kept the distribution business, and the stores joined a McKesson-owned banner.

The Pharmasave national group quickly realized that this was the tip of an iceberg. The threat of other stores leaving, combined with the substandard service they were receiving from their new distribution group, led them to cancel their contract and return to McKesson.

Then, as crazy as it sounds, I was criticized by several senior executives for overstepping my responsibilities, interfering with other departments, and not getting full approval before taking action. Luckily, the executives who mattered praised my team's efforts.

The last few years had been quite a ride. We now had a new state-of-the-art building in Moncton. The old Halifax and Moncton buildings were closed. We had almost closed the deal with Sobeys; we lost them but built the bridges we needed to ensure we could sign them in the future. McKesson was now running retail pharmacies. We had lost Pharmasave and then got them back. We moved twenty stores from Pharmasave to McKesson's Guardian Drug while always maintaining our high level of service in our core business. That's not to mention getting in trouble more times than I care to count

Sadly, we lost some friends and coworkers along the way, but despite all the change and uncertainty, morale and engagement never faltered. I was proud of our Atlantic group. With so many moving parts, everyone was still playing their role to perfection. As a result of our success, our confidence and reputation grew, and we felt like we could accomplish almost anything.

Is there a box?

The events described in this chapter are not for the faint of heart. All the back-and-forth was an incredible adrenaline rush. It was a scary and exciting time. I suppose I am the kind of guy who is at his best in the face of challenges when my atypical brain gets fired up.

The lessons I learned in this period of my life had a lot to do with not giving up and finding creative solutions to complicated problems. Sometimes, it's easy to say something just can't be done, but when you break problems into pieces, get out of the box, and engage the power of your team, solutions will usually float to the surface.

When asked about how they managed to think outside the box, a number of successful entrepreneurs offered the following answers:

- Doing the opposite of the expected
- Knowing who you are
- Involving employees
- Modifying what competitors are doing

- Doing the non-traditional[6]
- Exploring contradictory approaches
- Searching for recognizable patterns in disconnected domains[7]

I have to say that I have done all of those things at one point or another, but my approach often went further. I believe that sometimes you just have to ignore the box, maybe even give it a good kick, and understand that "boundary conditions are a choice."[8]

I was so stubborn and fixated on reaching my goals that I couldn't help but explore every possibility from every angle, over and over, until I found a path forward, even if that meant pissing off my colleagues or shaking up the status quo.

I found that having the willpower to stick to my approach and weather the shitstorm that was sure to come has been a vital element in my success.

Key takeaways

- Create your own opportunities.
- Jump the hurdles placed in front of you with enthusiasm.

LESSON 16

Live your entire life like there is no box

Hell, there are no rules here–we're trying to accomplish something.

Thomas Edison

During one of the many Digby Golf Classic events I attended, I had an interesting discussion with Dan White and his good friend Gordon Gilman, who worked for the New Brunswick Department of Health. Gordon was curious about my role and responsibilities at McKesson, what automation solutions we provided at Canadian and American hospitals, and how the New Brunswick hospitals were utilizing those services.

The conversation led to several subsequent meetings, when we looked at McKesson's footprint in the province and how those assets were being utilized. Surprisingly, the New Brunswick hospitals were loaded with McKesson automation. In fact, they were some of McKesson's best automation customers; who knew?

This wasn't due to great planning. It was the result of our salespeople being 'Johnny on the spot,' with a sixth sense to identify hospital administrators looking to spend their unused budget dollars. As a result of this haphazard approach to the purchasing and selling of automation, no operational or strategic plan was in place. This caused the hospitals' automation fill rates and efficiency to remain at substandard levels.

It also became apparent from our analysis that the hospitals were both over- and under-inventoried from having to use multiple vendors, various delivery methods, and high minimum orders. Essentially, Gordon's instincts were right: There was an obvious opportunity to improve efficiency, and McKesson likely had a role to play.

After some discussions with my superiors, Dan and I agreed to continue to manage the project for the moment. In my typical manner, I was ready to charge out of the gates and get 'er done. Understanding the way the system worked and sensing my impatient style, Gordon felt the need to give Dan and me a reality check on the way government works.

It went something like this: "You guys need to understand that regardless of how talented and wonderful you think you are, this project will take years to get done. Nothing will be easy, and the process will frustrate the hell out of you."

He elaborated. "Everyone in the system, at one time or another, has been burnt by some smooth-talking vendor who comes in with what they believe is the best and greatest idea, only to discover they are incapable of implementing it or it has fallen short of expectations. The result is a risk-averse system, where no one dares make a decision and everyone is waiting for someone else to sign off before giving their endorsement." As Gordon delivered his wisdom, Dan and I were looking at each other, thinking that maybe we should let the smart and politically-endowed people take this one. We were way out of my area of expertise. I knew nothing about automation, less about innovation, zero about hospitals or government, and my 'dog with a bone' approach might only serve to bite me in the ass.

At the same time, the other side of my brain was on fire, feeling the excitement of a big challenge and an opportunity to sink my teeth into something new. To be honest, I was naive enough to think that Gordon's warning didn't apply to me. I thought he just wasn't aware of my superpowers to get things done. Boy, would I be proven wrong!

Ignoring the naysayers

As none of the 'smart people' were lining up to take on the challenge, and my boss (Nick) liked the idea of my broadening my horizons, I agreed to give it a whirl. I started by meeting with the automation group. They told me I was wasting my time, assuring me that a province-wide solution was virtually impossible to implement anywhere in Canada. There were just too many layers of approval required, from individual hospitals, hospital groups, regional health authorities, health zones, and the Health Department, each with a board and CEO and countless layers of government on top of that. "Even if you beat the odds and get the hospitals and government to buy into the concept," they warned me, "then you have to get them to agree on the same governance, contract language, accountabilities, financial responsibilities, and so on." They concluded their 'motivational' speech with, "Good luck with that!" I thought, *Thanks for nothing!*

In all honesty, their comments didn't deter me one bit. If I altered course every time the smart people said I couldn't do something, I'd still be counting cards at bingo back on the Miramichi. No, wait, I got fired from that job. Well, you know what I mean—ha!

I wasn't sure where to begin. I didn't know anyone in government, but luckily, I knew someone who did. Lois Scott, who had just started working for McKesson, was well-connected in the New Brunswick political and hospital sectors after years of working within the provincial health care ecosystem. She had an amazing way about herself; she was loud, funny, and outspoken. She might be best described as a pit bull networker in heels.

Understanding the playing field

The first thing Lois told me was, "Rick, you need to understand that government is not one entity but many different groups of people with potentially very different agendas. If you want to get anything of significance done, you will need to engage all of them and address their individual concerns. You have the politician who wants to look good to the public to ensure votes; the bureaucrat, like the Deputy Minister, trying to keep everyone happy, balancing the wants of politicians with the needs of the hospitals; the professionals, like the Director of Nursing, trying to ensure professional standards and budgets are met, knowing very well that shit flows downhill; and the Premier's office, typically with a very separate agenda and reluctant to alienate any of the various stakeholders. They all talk about the need for change and innovation, knowing it is critical to improving healthcare. Yet, innovation means change, and change means risk, which they are all trying to avoid. This cycle ends up sending decision-making into a vacuum. That, my friend, is government!"

As I listened to Lois and recalled my little chat with Gordon, I started to realize that in addition to my lack of experience in this area, my style and personality seemed ill-equipped to deal with this political reality. I'd be like a duck climbing a tree with rubber boots on.

Before I could bail, though, Lois had me booked into a government reception the next frigging day. We figured, *What the hell; at least there'll be free booze.* And after listening to Lois and Gordon, God knows I needed a drink!

As I entered the reception room, Lois grabbed me by the ear like I was a three-year-old and said, "Ricky, you need to meet Mike Murphy, the Minister of Health." She dragged me across the room, and, in her deep, husky voice, shouted, "Mike, this is Ricky Brennan from McKesson. He runs Atlantic Canada and has lots of money. And he's a good Miramichi boy!"

Well, that felt weird. I shook Mike's hand, we had a quick chat about absolutely nothing, and away he went. Surprisingly and luckily, we ran into my cousin Mary Lou, who turned out to be the Minister's executive assistant. Who knew?

I also got reacquainted with Chris Collins, a member of the legislature from Moncton, who I knew from my Shoppers Drug Mart days. It was Chris who helped arrange a sit-down with the Minister to go over our concept. The Minister challenged us on a few points, but he was generally supportive. He advised us, "If you want to move this forward, the Directors of Nursing will have to buy in, and just so you know, with the scale of this project, it will take forever to get everyone to sign off on something like this!" I felt like telling him, "Yeah, yeah, I hear that a lot!"

The province had just been reduced to two health regions, which were in the process of amalgamation. This caused scads of people to slide into various roles. To our surprise, Gordon was named President of FacilicorpNB, the new Shared Service Organization. This was great news: a familiar face in a critical role. Unfortunately, Gordon's new position had limited practical benefit. As has been already made clear to the point of nausea, there were so many layers of approval that no individual, regardless of their position, could expedite a project of this scale.

Finding solutions

As we started to develop our concept, known as the Integrated Drug Supply Chain (IDSC), Dan and I spent countless hours with the Directors of Nursing and FacilicorpNB staff trying to validate their needs and ensuring our solution was the right one. Then, we ran the concept by the boards of the Health Regions, Pharmacy, Administration, Finance, Facility Management, and FacilicorpNB, and the Health Department. After about two years of this dog and pony show, we finally got all stakeholders to agree that the concept had merit. This allowed us to create a working group to assess the project's actual scope and its specific requirements. Each participant in the working group came with a list of needs and wants, which dramatically expanded the scope, complexity, and potential benefits of the project.

There seemed to be this feeling within the nursing group that it was time to right the ship. They believed that all patients and nurses in the province should have access to the same high quality of services, regardless of location or language. Their list had all the bells and whistles as well as the capability to significantly improve the quality of patient care while saving the hospital network substantial dollars.

Yet, the burning question at every meeting was, "How will the province afford to pay for the model with all the cutbacks?" It was at this moment that Dan and I jumped into action, shaking the corporate trees to find a solution. We convinced McKesson to eliminate the upfront capital and place the expense into the monthly service fee. This meant that the province would pay nothing upfront. Then, in conjunction with the health regions, we did a complete financial analysis of the potential savings (medication waste reduction, shrinkage, etc.), and lo and behold, the savings resulting from the various components of the model were greater than the monthly service fee. Our model would come at a net-zero cost to the province! Amazing!

I thought there would be a mad dash to get the contract signed, but oh, no. The no-risk mentality was so ingrained in the actions of every level of government that getting sign-off was still like pulling teeth. It was only after several more months of debate that I found a small group prepared to take a stand, and after five long years, we finally put pen to paper.

It was quite an accomplishment. The complexity, design, and scope of the model were staggering. It was the first of its kind anywhere, pieced together in our small corner of the world. It's incredible to think that for most of those years we worked on the IDSC, it was just a side project! We received no compensation; it wasn't even part of my formal performance review. Yet, as funny as it sounds, this lack of accountability had its benefits. Because it wasn't part of our jobs, no one was looking over our shoulder, hassling us, or complexifying the process.

This allowed us to take the time we needed to understand the customers' needs, pressure points, and constraints, which then allowed us to adapt the model to meet those needs while maximizing McKesson's investment.

Learning my way

I had gone from knowing nothing about hospitals, government, and complex automated pharmacy/hospital delivery systems to becoming an expert. I had benefited from having the freedom to learn my way—to ask questions, listen, discuss, and then toss the details around in my head until the pieces fell into place. It might have taken me longer to grasp the information, but when I finally got it, my brain locked onto it like a vice grip.

Then, I did what I do best: I rallied the troops, got the group organized, created a common vision, and then we attacked every piece with a certain stubborn enthusiasm, like a dog with a bone, until we knocked them off one by one. Dealing with the delays, the politics, and the countless layers of bureaucracy forced me to develop an unprecedented level of patience.

My constant exposure to CEOs and presidents, boards, and ministers made living in that world effortless. I began to feel surprisingly comfortable and free of the anxiety that so often held me back. Interestingly enough, the government and hospital executives I worked with were very similar to the execs I had encountered at McKesson: polished, intelligent, and diplomatic. These character traits had likely allowed them to rise through the ranks, but they were not much help when it came to getting anything accomplished.

As we moved into implementation, the knowledge, experience, and confidence I had gained over the previous number of years were critical to bringing the project to its successful completion. I just had to find the right people to get it done the right way.

Throughout this process, I learned a lot about breaking down barriers to innovation. Not in my wildest dreams had I imagined that stubborn, socially awkward me would end up learning how to talk to politicians and Health Department executives.

But there was something fresh about my approach. I didn't fear risk, I was not easily deterred, and I knew who to talk to when I needed to get things done. The whole experience taught me that no matter how insurmountable a task may appear or how many people tell you it can't be done, you just have to give it your all. I believe that one of the reasons we succeeded is that we truly listened to everyone. We had to listen; we didn't know anything and had no preconceived idea or commitment to a specific solution.

We championed the solution so fiercely that we collected new champions for our cause along the way. If we had been deterred by fear of the unknown, we would have never succeeded, not in a million years.

I once read that "risk-averse organizations often discard attractive projects before anyone formally proposes them."[9] I advocate the total opposite of that. In my career, I always jumped at the opportunity to explore challenging projects, regardless of risk, even if no one had the gumption to formally propose them. Having succeeded at making these massive bureaucratic bodies move their weighty armors all the way to the finish line gave me tremendous confidence that there was 'method in my madness.'[10]

Companies have become consumed by control, rules, and policies, causing creativity, initiative, and common sense to be ripped away from their very fabric. Then, to add to the dilemma, corporate leadership is defined by your willingness to follow those company rules, policies, and directives, further separating corporate leadership from what I would call real leadership.

This presents a challenge for us 'atypicals' as our skill set is never fully utilized when we are restricted by this gang-style, standardized rule book. Pushing the boundaries of the system will be critical to your success. You will have to find a way to balance your style and operating approach with corporate expectations—but don't worry, that's what we are good at. It won't always be easy, and you'll have to compromise, negotiate, and sometimes give in, but you'll usually find a way.

Key takeaways

- Not everyone will agree with your approach, and that's okay.
- Take pride in knowing that you are pushing boundaries.
- If you're listening, the answers are all around you.

LESSON 17

Done is better than perfect

You can do anything, but not everything.

David Allen

As we moved toward implementation of the Integrated Drug Supply Chain (IDSC), I focused on finding just the right team. I needed a disciplined yet flexible team capable of balancing the needs of multiple stakeholders, with enough backbone to stay strong as the inescapable corporate forces would come and try to complicate the process.

Building my team

My first hire would be Shirley Smallwood, Director of Citizen Engagement at the time for the New Brunswick Health Council. I had gotten to know her well over the years, and I knew she was the perfect candidate.

Shirley was conservative and more of a rule follower than I typically like, but she was loyal, smart, trustworthy, and had a calmness about her that could benefit me. These skills, I thought, would balance off my propensity to rush ahead without all the answers. She was also familiar with the people, the environment, and the bureaucracy, thanks to eighteen years of experience as a nurse at the Moncton hospital and five years working for the New Brunswick Department of Health.

We had been discussing the possibility of her joining my team for some time, and during the final stages of the interview process, Shirley felt compelled to inform me that she didn't have an MBA. She explained that if you had any hope of being promoted in government, you needed those types of credentials.

She was certainly surprised when I told her, "Well, thank God for that because I'm sure as shit not looking for someone who does. I need things to happen and don't have the time to get bogged down in needless analyses and what-ifs."

My comment led us to a discussion about my approach to business, including my 'done is better than perfect' (DIBTP) philosophy. Shirley quickly admitted that my seemingly haphazard approach to getting things done scared the hell out of her. She interpreted 'done is better than perfect' as cutting corners and not doing a good job. To make her point, she said, "Can you imagine a surgeon operating on a patient with a 'done is better than perfect' approach?"

My God, I almost coughed up a lung laughing at her comments.

I calmed her fears by explaining that 'done is better than perfect' doesn't mean not doing an excellent and thorough job. It means that we are in perpetual motion, doing what can be done, learning as we go, not letting the unknown or a conservative mindset bring us to a standstill.

"What I usually see," I said, "is that in an attempt to avoid risk and any potential negative outcomes, executives want every detail in place before they take the first step. It's like not pouring the foundation of your house because you haven't decided on the color of the roof shingles. Take our central fill pharmacy; no legislation allowed for the operating of one in New Brunswick. If I had waited for the Pharmacy Association to get around to developing the Central Fill guidelines, the IDSC project would have never happened."

It was the signing of the IDSC that prompted the Pharmacy Association to create the Central Fill Directive. We created our own success, and that's the real magic of 'done is better than perfect.'

I reassured my new hire that we were going to operate the central pharmacy and every other component of the IDSC model to the highest of standards. "However," I explained, "getting this project implemented will require this 'always moving forward' mindset." Once she understood my rationale, Shirley Smallwood agreed to come on board as the Director of the IDSC.

Together, we continued to build the team, promptly convincing Janet MacDonnell to head the central fill pharmacy component. I knew Janet well from my Shoppers Drug Mart days. Aside from being an experienced pharmacist with cutting-edge ideas about the business, it didn't hurt that she was well-acquainted with my straightforward management style. Janet was also an active member of the New Brunswick Pharmacy board, which would be invaluable considering there was no central fill pharmacy directive in place.

My third addition to the team was Dawn Steel in the role of project manager. She had previously worked with Rod Savoie, who gave her a big thumbs-up. According to Rod, she always spoke her mind. I thought that if she could handle Rod, she was exactly who I was looking for.

We completed our team by adding a few other highly-skilled individuals from the Atlantic team. And there it was: our IDSC team, a group of like-minded, positively-focused, straightforward, highly-skilled individuals.

They were all comfortable with my operational style and were able to slide into the large Moncton team with ease. As I had done with Shirley, I explained the 'done is better than perfect' philosophy to the team. I told them that we just couldn't afford to wait for every piece to be in place before moving forward; with so many unknowns, we'd just never get started.

Keeping it simple

Keeping it simple was at the core of our strategy. We broke the project into phases (avoiding the bells and whistles in the initial phases). Then, we divided the phases into sections, the sections into components, and the components into tasks. Finally, we broke each task into small, doable pieces.

As we discussed our game plan, I asked the team to explain every detail to me "like I'm an eight-year-old." Then, we dug deep into the operational guts of every component, ensuring that everyone understood the task at hand, their role, everyone else's role, and how they were interconnected. I listened to the conversations, observed everyone's body language, and only let the discussion end when I saw the proverbial light bulb go on for every single team member. These detailed discussions, especially in the earlier meetings, were critical to establishing accountability and ensuring each team member's understanding of how their efforts fit into the big picture.

Don't confuse this approach with complexifying the process. It was quite the opposite; we moved quickly and kept things simple. There were no deep analyses, no prolonged debates, no endless meetings. We just focused on making sure things were clear and organized. We would then identify the gaps, agree on a temporary fix and timeline, enlist the appropriate product experts to work on the solutions, and push on, doing what we could and learning as we went.

Of course, things could sometimes go sideways. Being in perpetual motion and moving forward without all the answers has its obvious disadvantages.

Many executives would argue that these problems could be avoided with more time, analysis, and planning, and that's the trap so many fall into!

The fear of making a mistake, the thought of looking less than perfect, and the lack of experience dealing with risk keep most model executives inside the safe corporate box. This 'protect your ass' mindset slows execution to a snail's pace, leading to increased costs, delays, and a hell of a lot of frustration.

To minimize any possibility of real risk, we dissected the project into small, manageable pieces, learned to fix things quickly, and ensured the customers were well-informed. Then, we set our priorities, ensuring the end users (the nurses) were on board.

Change is always hard, but in this case, it was harder! We were dealing with almost 10,000 nurses in countless facilities spread across a province who spoke two different languages and were overworked, short-staffed, and pissed off at the bureaucracy and cutbacks.

The implementation process would involve persuading those nurses to adopt a model that would change almost every aspect of their working life. Ensuring they understood how the model would make their life easier and improve patient care was paramount. So, while other VPs were fixated on creating spreadsheets, in-depth analyses, and fancy presentations, our team was out in the trenches, training, educating, and listening.

Too many cooks spoil the broth

As the project gained momentum, it became an important part of the company's financial outlook. As expected, the Senior Executive Group wanted more visibility. I told my boss we'd be happy to provide whatever information and data they required. Unfortunately, they had another idea. They wanted an 'official' steering committee to provide guidance and oversight, the very thing I was hoping to avoid!

All too often, I've seen these 'steering' committees kill the momentum of a project as if they were throwing out an anchor, thus slowing down the process and leading to vast amounts of needless work, unnecessary complexity, diluted accountabilities, and financial creep.

Over the next year, my worst nightmare was realized when my team was forced to waste countless hours creating charts, presentations, and spreadsheets (in just the right way); performing analyses; and creating meaningless benchmarks. All this energy wasn't meant to improve the product, its implementation, or the customer experience, but to satisfy the steering committee's erroneous demands.

The budget was never out of line, the timelines were never off schedule, and the customers were never unhappy, yet the demands of the steering committee never ceased.

Then, to add to the dysfunction, the Supply Solutions group, which was responsible for hospital activity across the country, sent their new VP to Moncton to lend us a helping hand. She was an engineer by trade—intelligent, well-spoken, and in total alignment with the steering committee's methodology.

Upon her arrival, she immediately put the team off-center, making disparaging remarks and opposing almost everything the team was doing. This caused nothing but stress and confusion.

Interestingly, when she discussed employees with other executives, she did so very respectfully, giving the impression that she was employee-focused. Yet, the reality was that she treated employees with total disregard. She never raised her voice or used inappropriate language. She made her less-than-nice comments in a soft voice and with a smile. Her demeanor became a big joke around the office: "You can be as mean as you want; just do it with a smile!"

Over the next several months, the VP of Supply Solutions was relentless, continually badgering the team, coercing them to change their operating practices and adopt her preferred project tools. She didn't understand why we were putting so much time and effort into the nurses; she thought that was the government's problem to solve.

Meanwhile, the concept of 'done is better than perfect' almost drove her out of her mind! I tried to neutralize her as best I could, but I didn't have the authority to send her packing. She had the ear of a couple of the SVPs on the steering committee, so I knew if I pushed too hard, it would only come back to bite me in the ass.

The growing subculture

My team was struggling to understand how senior management could condone her conduct. From what they saw, the company's leadership seemed committed to employee engagement, always taking the time to hold leadership events and town hall meetings and continually speaking about how employees were our 'greatest asset.' Yet, there was an obvious disconnect between their words and actions. It became clear that the appearance of culture was far more important than actually having a strong culture!

The company's top executives seemed to be blind to the fact that each employee's day-to-day interactions with their superiors shaped their experience of the corporate culture. Whether those interactions were positive or negative, respectful or demeaning, empowering or confrontational was much more important to creating a culture than the descriptions of that culture in fancy speeches and employee handbooks.

As I discussed my observations with my peers around the country, I sensed there was a silent movement afoot. Attitudes were shifting, and people were becoming more guarded and politically sensitive.

Employees were acting like they were happy when they were not. They said they supported the companies directions, but their body language said something else. I often noticed senior managers mumbling negative remarks after a presentation or when certain people entered a room.

This subculture that was emerging was invisible to most of our executives, hidden in the background or behind a crooked smile, only showing its face in the form of low productivity, slow execution, hidden resentment, and key talent leaving the company.

As the situation with the new VP of Supply Solutions evolved, it became a clear example of the cultural contradiction. Her behavior with employees was ignored and the disruptions to the project justified, largely because she spoke the executive language and was able to tell the higher-ups what they wanted to hear, creating a narrative that rationalized her actions.

It went so far that Alain, my boss, was browbeaten into talking to me about my perceived lack of professionalism and uncooperative nature and was ultimately forced to lower my performance rating. Having great respect for Alain, I took his remarks as constructive criticism and agreed to watch my words, but as I do in most situations like this, I went on the offensive.

Sure, I was less vocal and outwardly difficult, but I took firmer control of the project, instructing the team to continue per my direction. If anyone had concerns, I asked them to send them to me. *Let me deal with them with a soft voice and a smile,* I thought. Ha! Not my style, but I had to adapt to survive.

In the end, the team implemented the project flawlessly, on time, on budget, and our way. The model we built and implemented was world-class, with automated dispensing units in every nursing ward in every hospital in the province, delivering prepackaged, individually barcoded medication coming straight from a fully-automated central fill pharmacy. The new system also featured biometrics scanning to track the movement of medication by each nurse, consolidated and just-on-time inventory, complex price management software, and the option to do patient bedside barcoded verification to ensure the right drug got to the right patient at the right time. That's not all; the IDSC project was the biggest automation deal in McKesson Canada's history.

You never know who is watching

We put up with a lot of crap through the IDSC years, worst of all from executives who thought they had all the answers and added complexity at every turn while ignoring the inappropriate actions of a senior manager just because she spoke their language.

Through this period of exceptional performance and innovation, I would be personally raked over the coals for being too rough and assertive, uncompromising, and unprofessional.

Yet, despite the negative narrative, drama, contradictory messaging, and corporate infighting, other executives were taking note of our accomplishments and our ability to jump the hurdles put in front of us by both external and internal forces.

I came to realize that the traits that made me unpopular with some executives were the very same that gave me great credibility with others.

My 'done is better than perfect' (DIBTP) approach was, in many ways, the key to my success. Simple and easy to understand and manage, it lined up perfectly with how my brain worked. Complexity confused and frustrated the hell out of me, meetings bored me, uncertainty gave me anxiety, and political agendas drove me mad. This led me to create a system that simplified and clarified everything, and did it ever work! It unleashed the true potential of my teams, allowing us to knock off one accomplishment after another to the praise of some executives and the astonishment of others. Through thick and thin, I always stood behind my team, and our commitment to one another was never shaken.

We were trying to achieve the impossible, and the finish line was in sight. But there was no fairy-tale ending. As we were hard at work on implementing the IDSC, a lot was happening behind the scenes, and it wouldn't take long for me to find out what they were.

Key takeaways

- Simplicity and clarity are essential to high-performing teams.
- Willingly accept risk.
- Don't allow others to complexify the process.

LESSON 18

I tried, but I just couldn't stop learning!

A man who carries a cat by the tail learns something he can learn no other way.

Mark Twain

I always thought I knew what was going on around me, especially when someone was spinning a web, had a hidden agenda, or was just full of shit. Well, I was about to find out that words and actions were never quite what they seemed. Every decision was cleverly wrapped in executive self-interest, while good intentions were hijacked by the perceived needs of business and the lure of personal financial rewards.

As I entered the senior management world, many of my peers told me that compromising your personal beliefs for the good of the company was at the heart of corporate leadership. Frankly, I thought that was total bull. The leaders I respected seemed to have a more balanced approach. Sure, they sometimes compromised on the little stuff, allowing others to win the non-essential battles, but they rarely, if ever, compromised on the important stuff.

One day, as the IDSC project was gaining traction, Nick told me, "Rick, now that you've done the hard stuff, people will be coming out of the woodwork to get involved in the project for their own benefit. Don't let them; they'll only fuck it up!"

Nick got the nuances of the system. He knew when to charge ahead, when to relinquish control, and when to hold firm. It was precisely this wisdom that allowed him to accomplish something pretty remarkable: leapfrog his boss and the rest of the Canadian Executive Team (CET) to be named President of McKesson Canada.

The news rocked the company. To the best of my knowledge, Nick managed to get to the top without compromising his core values, relationships, or commitments. Impressive! It was great news for me. Nick and I had a solid relationship, and one of the first things he did in his new role was to expand the country into four regions, creating a stand-alone Atlantic division. This new structure gave me a promotion to Regional VP for Atlantic Canada. The move put me on the senior management team and had me reporting directly to Alain, the National SVP of Operations.

Nick's decision took guts; the U.S. brass and the CET were dead set against it. To be honest, their views had merit; we all knew that McKesson Canada would move to a national structure over the next eighteen months, meaning that the position he had just given me would be eliminated.

But Nick had a plan. He wanted me to experience and learn the ins and outs of the senior management world. Now, it was up to me to learn quickly. I started working with Alain, who was smart, open-minded, and always available. We quickly developed a strong working relationship of our own. We would experience a lot together over those eighteen months, including the turmoil surrounding the IDSC implementation.

Then, as expected, McKesson Canada announced it was moving to a national structure. Luckily, before the official announcement, I got a call from Alain advising me that I had a new role—are you ready for this?—as the National VP of Supply Solutions. I nearly shit myself. After all the criticism, harassment, and second-guessing that my team and I had endured through the IDSC implementation, they were firing my antagonist and giving me her job? How does that make any sense?

When my team heard the news of her demise, half of them went into shock, and the other half were doing cartwheels down the hall. She was supposedly the golden child of several of the SVPs, and she and HR seemed to be kindred spirits. So, what had gone wrong for her?

I had to know more, so I badgered Alain for answers, and while he was too professional to get into the details, he did offer that essentially, when it came time to make big decisions, the higher-ups were forced to cut through the hype and get to the facts, choosing my results over her spin and leadership over political acumen.

Alain also shared that at various times throughout his career, he too had gotten heat for doing what he believed to be in the best interest of the company, and it was during those times that he clung to his core beliefs and carried on as best he could, just as I had done. His key message was clear: You can't win every battle, so you need to pick your fights or you may not win the ones that matter, a concept I completely understood.

I'd speak up, but no one's listening

Once I started attending senior management meetings, I was surprised at how little real participation or debate took place. Sure, people spoke here and there, but it was just meaningless banter and a lot of ass-licking. They seemed to be afraid that any negative comment might be perceived as offensive or as a sign of a poor attitude. So, everyone was careful with what they said and how they said it.

What blew me away was that these were the same people who, outside the meeting room, had balls the size of coconuts and freely shared their frustrations with the company. Yet, they sat there in silence, smiling like they had a stick up their butt, laughing at the CET's jokes, unwilling or unable to voice their true opinions.

This silence gave the executive team the impression that everyone was happy and on the same page. Yet, nothing could have been further from the truth. The silence and politeness were not signs of commitment or buy-in but rather symptoms of a compromised culture.

Apparently, for the executive team, it was easier to accept the smiles at face value than to dig deeper and confront the team on the inconsistency between their words and actions.

It was hard for me to relate to this environment. My team meetings had always been full of debate. Everyone challenged everything, sometimes aggressively, and we would all just laugh about it later. I'd go as far as to say that our enthusiastic exchange and banter were at the heart of our team cohesion; everything was on the table, like it or not.

Fear of failure vs. desire to win

As I trained myself to endure these dreadful executive meetings, Alain suggested that I should retain an executive coach, which was trendy at the time. Undoubtedly, the idea had come from the HR crowd, who had more than frowned upon my feud with my predecessor at the helm of Supply Solutions.

I must confess I was pretty uncomfortable with the idea of a coach at first, but I quickly learned to embrace the experience. My coach's guidance was logical, straightforward, and, most importantly, confidential, which allowed us to speak truthfully.

As we dug into my background, examined my accomplishments, and evaluated my priorities, he quickly picked up one particular personality trait that was guiding my every action: my fear of failure. As we explored this revelation, he helped me understand that although my approach got things done, it triggered in me and others, certain negative emotions and a hell of a lot of anxiety. He suggested that I flip my focus to a desire to win, which could ease my anxiety and send me down a more constructive path while still allowing me to accomplish my objectives.

This new insight prompted me to look back at my life: sports championships, performance numbers, promotions, and personal milestones. I came to the realization that I had rarely felt the joy of winning, only a deep sense of relief from not losing.

I started working hard to adjust my mindset in an attempt to better appreciate the pleasures of life, friends, family, and coworkers. This gave me a new measure of success. I may have acted the same way on the surface after the coaching, yet, inside, I was calmer, my anxiety diminished, and I learned to better appreciate the little things that life had to offer.

Then, as it usually happens in big companies, things started to change. Nick moved on to a bigger and better job in the U.S. Alain became President. Paula Keays took his job, and a very special role became available: SVP of Retail Banner Services. It was the perfect role for me, but it wouldn't be easy to get it.

Going for my dream job

Other executives with more political clout would undoubtedly be going hard after it, including the SVP of HR, who had made her intentions clear that she wanted to run a business unit. I'm sure that few saw me as a real contender in those early days; most were unaware of my retail background, and my style was a far cry from the Armani-wearing, fine-wine-loving executive type. Yet, undaunted, with the odds stacked against me, I started to prepare.

The first thing I did was go see my old friend, Johnny Mac, who now owned several stores in the McKesson network with Guardian. With the help of his business manager, Shawn Hulshof, we evaluated the strengths, weaknesses, and glaring holes in the McKesson Retail Banner group and its banner stores. We created a new strategy, one that would fill in those holes and reorganize the four banners and office into one state-of-the-art Shared Service Organization.

What I was proposing wasn't anything new; the structure was commonly used in the retail industry, and the tools were widely available and cheap. The reality was that the McKesson Banner Group and the stores were so far behind the times that the fix wasn't that difficult if you knew where to look. So, what seemed innovative was only innovative to us, but for now, that would do the trick.

My second move was updating my wardrobe. This was inspired by comments like Dick Peterson's ("I don't need to worry about what I wear to a meeting if Rick's going; I'm sure to look better than him") and Paula Keays's jokes about my oversized suits and outdated looks. So, off I went to buy skinny pants, skinny suits, and other skinny accessories to look more the part.

Finally, I prepared for the interviews, enlisting the help of my executive coach, who would be instrumental in helping me showcase my abilities.

Most importantly, he helped me understand how my answers would be interpreted. He explained that my answers would matter more than my performance history; they would want to hear me be assertive and show outward confidence. To them, that would show leadership. I thought to myself, *What a crock; words over actions, once again.*

I knew that trying to sell myself with words wouldn't play to my strengths. While I am assertive as hell and can get things done like no one else, my ability to tell my tale would pale in comparison to the velvet-tongued executives I'd be competing against. If I hoped to be successful in my quest, my new vision and my reorganization plan would have to be the cornerstone of my story.

When the time for the interviews came, I was well-rehearsed and had my strategy well-planned. At each interview, I took the interviewer through my plan, making sure they understood my logic, its financial impact, and my in-depth knowledge of the retail pharmacy business. I was hoping this would counterbalance the advantages my polished and well-connected competitors had over me.

It was a long, drawn-out process, yet my plan and my knowledge of how to pull it off gave me the advantage I was hoping for, and I was offered the job, contingent on passing the mandatory tests. Yikes!

Yes, I'd been with the company for years, but the HR leadership insisted on the testing "for your own good," they told me, to ensure the job "isn't too much for me." Can you imagine?

Behind the curtain

As you already know, my learning disabilities would make it impossible for me to do well on these tests. As expected, my results came back with countless red flags. HR jumped all over them, concluding that I lacked certain leadership, assertiveness, and team-building skills, the very characteristics that I'd built a career on!

But by then, Alain was likely convinced that I was the person for the job, and he insisted that the lead psychologist of the recruitment firm interview me to get his opinion. In anticipation, I discussed my upcoming meeting with my coach, who prepared me for "the trap question." He explained, "This is the first thing to watch for, especially if someone doesn't want you to get this job: They'll try and convince you to take another job that they 'all' feel is better suited for you."

He further explained, "It's all about your answers; be firm and confident as you reject their offer."

I went to the psychologist's office, and we went over my test results. I explained the way I understood the questions and why I answered as I did, which he seemed to accept without issue. Then came the trap question, to which I firmly replied, "This is the only job for me; no other option will be considered."

My answer sealed the deal. The psychologist told Alain that my answers were reflective of the personality profile required for the job, and I was offered the position.

There is no doubt that without my coach's insights and Alain's persistence, I would have never got the job. There were just too many other factors and conflicting interests at play. While my experiences, successes, and capabilities were well-documented, it was the answers to the predetermined questions that seemed to prove my competency.

Somehow, over the years, HR used the testing process to hijack and gain total control of who was hired by the company. The tool was used as the ultimate decision-making device, one that was not to be questioned.

Look at my situation: I had been with the company for fourteen years, I knew everyone, my accomplishments were many, I'd had the best personal performance rating in the company on multiple occasions, my employee engagement scores were always top-tier, and my financial and operational results never faltered. Yet, HR could still convince senior management that I lacked the very qualities they saw me demonstrate on countless occasions based on the dot I colored in on a piece of paper. Beyond ridiculous!

Let's face it: The system is geared to keeping everything the same. Leadership is defined and measured by a cast of bureaucrats and executives who often talk about the need for change, strong leadership, and bringing new types of thinkers into the company, yet quickly disqualify them for their lack of experience and 'professionalism,' or for not coloring the right dot.

I am not suggesting that testing, behavioral interviews, and such aren't valuable tools. They are, but only when used as single pieces of a comprehensive hiring puzzle.

I've seen the same crooked rationale used in so many initiatives the company has sponsored over the years. Take diversity. The idea is wonderful, wrapped with good intentions and fancy mission statements as companies set out to hire people of different colors, sexual orientations, ethnic backgrounds, and so on. Yet, when diversity hiring takes place, the search is on for people who do indeed come from those sectors of the population but whose thinking is consistent with the prevailing executive mindset (the corporate personality profile), which nullifies the advantages that real diversity might bring.

As I write these words, I realize I do so through the eyes of a white middle-class male who can't possibly understand the challenges faced by other sectors and backgrounds of the population. Yet, I do understand that overcoming the challenges that life presents creates wisdom and a unique perspective that can benefit every company.

But, let's face it, executives want things to be easy, and too much diversity of thought is a pain in the ass. To them, having to accommodate opposing points of view may be a social requirement, but, in reality, they see it as only slowing down the machine.

Take me, for example. Although I don't belong to any of the targeted diversity groups, my limitations, disabilities, and corresponding management style led me to take a very different approach to business. Regardless of how effective I was and how many accomplishments I stockpiled, my style came very close to keeping me out of the senior executive ranks.

As evidence of this, in more than fourteen years with the company, I was never invited to the annual executive talent sessions for 'highly promotable' managers. Sure, I was a keeper, a street-smart dude who got things done, but not someone they wanted sitting around the senior executive table talking about my favorite grape and vineyard at the executive retreats.

That's the way the executive ecosystem works. They want people who are a fit, who share the same interests and have the same outlook. The problem is that this keeps everything the same, preventing companies from maximizing the power of diversity and, most importantly, diversity of thought.

With so much effort put into avoiding change in the company, I knew I had to watch my step as I moved into my new role. I knew I'd have to buck the system just enough to give my plan a chance of success and my team the wiggle room to get things done.

By this time in my career, I knew how to meet my objectives and bring in the numbers, but I still had a lot to learn about the executive mindset and how to work successfully in that environment. I had become used to being on the other side of popular opinion, but I knew that too much of that would surely put me on the losing end in my new world.

My challenge would be to stay true to my moral code, operating style, and team philosophy while not alienating my new CET colleagues. I had a few friends in the CET and a strong relationship with my boss (the president), so I listened to their advice and adjusted my plans accordingly.

I would learn from my new coach about the different personality profiles in the executive group, from the make-it-happen types who had little need for praise to the socialites with a big appetite for the spotlight and the scientist types who needed vast amounts of information before making any decision. These differences resulted in each one having a different perspective on life and leadership.

My coach explained that if I wanted to be successful, I would have to find a way to work with each personality type effectively. As a result,

I took the time to understand each individual's thinking and motivations before dealing with each executive in a way that I thought they would best respond to. For the most part, it worked, so make a point of understanding who you're working with, and adapt accordingly.

Key takeaways

- Heed the advice of those you trust.
- Remember that stubbornness and persistence are virtues.

LESSON 19

Never compromise who you are

It is easier to fool people than to convince someone they have been fooled.

Mark Twain

The opportunity that lay in front of me was everything I had ever dreamed of. It was a real opportunity to demonstrate my abilities at the highest level of the corporation. But what got me charged up was the chance to show that my skills and operational style trumped those of the smooth-talking, politically-savvy executives who the corporation seemed to be fixated on.

As my appointment was announced, there were varying reactions. Some were surprised, even a little shocked. Meanwhile, there was a real sense of excitement from the general employee population. It wasn't only about my personal accomplishment; there was a sense of optimism that someone outside of the typical smooth-talking, fork-tongued executive stereotype could rise to this level in the company.

As the news spread throughout the industry, I received several congratulatory emails and phone calls from business acquaintances. One heartfelt note took me back to my Shoppers days, inspiring me and reminding me that I can do whatever I set my mind to.

March 24, 2015

Hi Rick,

Dan sent me an email about your appointment as Senior Vice President of Retail at McKesson. Congratulations! We are not surprised that you have built an excellent career with the McKesson organization. You and John Mac elevated Shoppers Drug Mart Atlantic to the best operating region in the country. The best compliment I ever heard was from Jean Coutu when he visited every SDM across the country. He said, "The only region that knew what they were doing and how to run stores was Atlantic Canada." This was during your and John's reign, and I attribute Coutu's remarks directly to your efforts. A great compliment to you both.

Again, congratulations! And all the best in your new position, where I know you will be very successful. Hope all is well with you and your family.

Best regards,

Ed Parker

VP Marketing, Shoppers Drug Mart, Atlantic

Ed was a mentor to us young guys back in the day, always positive and one of the few executives I've known in my career with a genuine, contagious enthusiasm. He never played at being an 'executive' like we saw so many others do. He was just himself—an abstract thinker, honest, smart, and kind, and we loved him for it. He used to call us the 'young lions.' Ha!

My first order of business as Senior VP of Retail was to sell my plan to my management team. I made it clear that we needed to move fast, be bolder, and be extremely creative if we hoped to transform the business in any meaningful way.

This wouldn't be easy. McKesson was primarily a distribution company, and it approached problem-solving and change through a cautious, conservative lens. Decisions were carefully thought out, issues were analyzed in depth, committees were formed, and rules and processes were established to ensure one standardized approach.

However, I knew there was no time to be careful and safe. We had to resort to my good ol' 'done is better than perfect' approach if we had any hope of catching up to our competitors and resetting our trajectory. I also knew that if I played it safe, it wouldn't be long before the naysayers began asking, "What the hell has Rick accomplished anyway?"

Understand what success looks like to you

The corporate pharmacies and other independent chains were eating our lunch, and we had none of the tools or expertise to bring about the changes required. On top of that, pharmacy margins were dropping due to legislative changes; costs were rising, and stores were leaving our banners for our competitors. Speed would be critical; there was no time to mess around, and that meant taking some calculated risks.

But first things first. I needed to understand what was going on around me. I started by walking around the office every morning, chatting with the staff, trying to get to know them and learn about their concerns. It was clear that the physical environment sucked. The office was cluttered and dirty, with hundreds of boxes lined up and down every hallway. Meanwhile, the employees struggled to understand their roles, how decisions were made, and in what direction the retail business was headed.

Even the simplest tasks were difficult. The keypad on the employee entrance had been broken for six months. Each morning, through wind, rain, and snow, employees had to bang relentlessly on the door in hopes that someone would let them in, which pissed them off to no end. When I questioned why, I was told by the person responsible that he had not received the required written approval to fix the problem. Managing to contain myself and not blow a gasket, I immediately picked up the phone, called a locksmith, gave him my credit card, and had the keypad fixed the next day.

This simple act echoed through the building as if I had slain a giant, sending a clear message that things were about to change. It was painfully evident that the idea of initiative and pride in one's work had systematically been ripped away and replaced by this blind obedience to the rules that came from above.

As I dug deeper, I discovered that most employees were working hard, yet they were bogged down in meetings and phone calls that had little or nothing to do with our business or their jobs. This had to stop! I asked the team to start declining non-retail-related meetings, which threw most of them into convulsions. They thought I'd lost my mind! At this point, I was more than prepared to battle it out with my new team. Their idea of accountability and their sense of priorities were way off base, and that had to change.

McKesson was all about meetings, and not accepting a meeting request was a foreign concept to most. It took some time and more than a few debates, but the idea of being accountable for one's time and performance eventually took hold, and we all got moving in the right direction.

Then, McKesson Canada announced the purchase of RemedyRX, a pharmacy group comprising 250 stores and a corporate staff that needed to be absorbed into our group. Halfway through the transition, we started moving the Remedy talent into key management positions, identifying the nonperformers in our own business and promoting our performers.

Fighting executive ego and bureaucracy

Next, we went to the market to find the missing pieces of my talent puzzle. I knew where to find at least one of those pieces: Shawn Hulshof, who had helped me prepare for my interviews along with Johnny Mac. In Shawn, I recognized a deep knowledge of retail and a clear understanding of where the gaps lay within the Guardian Banner and the Retail Banner groups. Having him on board would save me years of trying to figure it out on my own.

I had called HR during my first week as SVP to kickstart Shawn's interview process, which was typically a long, drawn-out ordeal. He had no problem with the Pathfinder testing. He sailed through his interviews with the president and most of the SVPs. That was until the last interview with none other than the SVP of HR. She decided she didn't like some of his answers to her questions and refused to sign off. This was odd, even for her; Shawn had all the qualifications. He was well-known, had been highly recommended, and had aced HR's beloved test.

What frustrated me was how she could think that she knew—better than me—who I could work with effectively. Most likely, she was just flexing her muscle, trying to show me who was running the show. Who knows?

Nonetheless, I insisted on hiring Shawn. Oh, but the HR SVP was a hard nut, and she held firm on her assertion that he wasn't the right candidate. "I've been around a long time," she told me, "and you can trust my instincts. I'm rarely wrong." Can you imagine? The situation forced me to have a serious conversation with our boss, Alain, about who was running my business unit.

This was my introduction to the senior level of the executive world, where ego and intimidation ran amok, and humility was nowhere to be found.

Yes, I finally got Shawn hired, but I had to compromise; there was always a compromise. In this case, they let me hire him at a reduced level and salary, but I figured I'd deal with that later.

The HR leadership would never forgive my insubordination, and as a result, my every move came under her watchful eye. By the way, Shawn became a critical part of the team, someone I relied on almost every day. His category management team was key to transforming the business, becoming the majority contributor to the RBG profit bucket. So much for her instincts!

The situation with Shawn and the HR SVP was such an eye-opener. It made me realize that my idea of what a team should be was very different from the perspective of other executives. To me, a team is like a puzzle. Each one is different, containing pieces of various shapes and sizes, and when you put the pieces together in just the right way, a unique and wonderful image comes to life.

In my case, I needed people with certain personality traits and skill sets to balance off my shortcomings. I needed to surround myself with people who could challenge me, stand up for their point of view, run with the ball, take risks, and not be so damn politically correct.

While the standard approach might be in line with HR policies and testing might ensure a profile consistent with HR expectations, it would do nothing to help me build the team I needed to succeed.

Creating opportunity

As the team came together and I moved forward with the plan, we soon ran into our first major roadblock. It seemed that we didn't have the money to finance our redesign, and there was no appetite to go to corporate (in the U.S.) for funding. The financial realities forced us to take a step back and take a hard look at the business. Digging deep, we examined everything we did and how we did it.

This resulted in some bold moves, which shook the business to its bones and yielded millions! With the funding now in hand, we achieved a staggering amount over a short period, impressing most. But not everyone would be a fan. IT wanted to build and control our tools, and the Distribution group wanted to layer more costs onto our stores to their own advantage. Finance wanted to take the savings directly to the annual bottom line, and HR was constantly trying to force us to slow down and adhere to traditional distribution protocols.

Undaunted, and with the support of my boss, I pushed forward. I hired the required talent and bought and reconfigured the industry tools. The transformation would be swift, dramatically improving our service, sometimes going from 'no service' in an area to 'best in class' overnight!

The Pharmacy department was our main focus. After all, we were a pharmacy company, and it wasn't long before we went from having no full-time pharmacists in the office to eighteen and a full support staff servicing all banners. We then repeated the process with every other department until we had a full stable of staff, tools, and services.

Taking the time to have fun

All of this was great, but I knew that if we were going to hit it out of the park, achieving a higher level of employee engagement was the critical piece to the puzzle. We had already cleaned up the work environment and transitioned out the employees who were not pulling their weight. We got organized, making sure that everyone was accountable and that objectives were clear and simple. However, I could tell that the team was still feeling the stress and pressure that change brings, and I knew we had to balance it off with a little fun.

Keep in mind that my definition of fun had changed considerably over the years. I had become gluten- and dairy-free. I had also stopped drinking beer and wine, a self-imposed punishment for my decades of abuse

The people I worked with at this point only knew the duller version of Rick, and when I shared a story about living a life in full party mode, they just smiled, thinking to themselves, "Sure, old man!"

Nonetheless, I still understood the value of fun and creating a relaxed work environment. With the help of a reactivated social committee, we organized summer barbecues, food trucks, ice cream deliveries, Christmas coffee and cupcake carts, chili cookoffs, and various other activities.

The next step was to enhance every single employee's day-to-day experience by ensuring that managers were organized and treated their subordinates with respect. When they didn't, we held them accountable. I made it my mission, especially in that first year, to walk around the office every morning, saying hello and chatting with the team while observing their body language. I'd often take employees out to lunch to dig deeper, ensuring as best I could that I had a clear sense of what was going on in the building.

Our management team went out for dinner every other month and held quarterly off-site meetings, including one memorable reunion at my New Brunswick cottage. The cottage had a bunkhouse and enough room to accommodate everyone—well, if you weren't too picky.

We reviewed our numbers, goals, and priorities and even enjoyed some karaoke. But my main objective at that meeting was to get the team to talk about us: our relationships, our interactions, and the level of cooperation within the group. I had arranged for someone to start the conversation by challenging an aspect of my leadership style. I was hoping this would spark discussion, and it did! As the flood of concerns began, people spoke about gaps in communication, priority misalignment between groups, and how a lack of trust and transparency was holding us back as a team. They opened up about how the simplest email could be misinterpreted and how certain managers were holding employees to a lower standard of performance than others, fostering inequities and hard feelings.

This open discussion hit the mark; it made us rethink our approach and inspired us to find new ways to ensure that our group's actions were more aligned with the strategies of other groups within RBG.

These off-site meetings, open discussions, and team activities were critical in creating the atmosphere I was looking for, one that would allow us to stop, take a breath, have a little fun, and try to understand each other just a little better.

For the sake of my mental health, I needed to take time for myself to refocus, regain my perspective, clear my mind, and neutralize my anxiety. It was almost like the more relaxation time I took, the more valuable I was to the company. In fact, throughout my career, I never worked long hours and never missed the chance to go home early or take a vacation. This was in stark contrast to my fellow executives, who believed that they should be seen pounding away late at night or early in the morning. I just never found any truth in that. It seemed that when my teams felt happy, respected, and fulfilled, they didn't care where I was or what I was doing. In fact, they often told me to go away and play and "let us do our jobs!"

My focus was on getting things done, so I didn't waste my time doing things or putting on a charade that had no value.

In my new role, I spent considerable time with the Executive Group, where they often said to me, "We're your new team now," almost as if the Retail team for which I was responsible was secondary to my commitment to the CET. This struck me as odd because we only saw each other occasionally, we had different and sometimes opposing objectives, and their operating methods and their approach to teamwork were light-years apart from my own. To be honest, these self-proclaimed teammates of mine were often my greatest obstacles.

Throughout my career, I had developed and mastered a particular operational system. I relied on simplicity and clarity, and I knew that a motivated team was essential to my success. When I moved to Toronto, I was asked to attend meetings with my executive counterparts and lay out my plans to generate executive input. Almost instinctively, they tried to add complexity and set up a reporting schedule and steering committee. They saw my need for speed and my 'done is better than perfect' approach as counterintuitive to the actions of a 'mature' executive.

Sensing executive interference on the horizon and wanting to ensure that my team had the runway to achieve our goals, I opted for the following approach:

1) I advised my team not to share information with other business units until we could properly lay out the concept, action plan, benefits, and financial rationale.
2) I tempered my information sharing with the CET, giving them enough to satisfy their inquiries but not enough to draw them into our activities.
3) I made sure my boss (who was also their boss) was well informed in advance of my actions and progress to circumvent any misleading narratives.

These actions seemed to work, allowing us to charge ahead and accomplish our objectives

Key takeaways

- Get out of meetings, stop talking, and actually do something.
- Balance transparency with partiality.

LESSON 20

The Leadership Façade

Behind every glorious façade, there is always hidden something ugly.

Stanislaw Lem

Soon after I joined the senior executive ranks, I got to see firsthand how my new teammates balanced the pressures of the corporate world and the leadership values expected of them. This balancing act often resulted in them saying one thing, doing another, and thinking something entirely different.

From the company's perspective, as long as performance was strong and leadership values were seemingly on display, they assumed everything was great and let the Canadian executive team do their thing.

It was quite a show at times, with executives acting and talking like leaders yet rarely demonstrating the leadership values that the company posted on every wall and flaunted at every meeting. This was the moment I came to understand the 'leadership façade' that was playing out in front of my eyes.

Just like actors in a movie, these façade-focused leaders projected an outward image that oozed confidence, enthusiasm, and charisma; they learned to speak well in public, dressed well, and always knew the right thing to say. They were constantly posing as advocates for diversity, philanthropy, ethics, and teamwork.

It was astonishing to watch, and the façade worked like a charm, causing the company brass and many employees to define leadership by the traits they saw masterfully executed. However, it wouldn't be long before employees who were directly in the line of fire became frustrated with the gaping holes between their words and actions.

This disconnect only got worse when business pressure came to bear, personal performance ratings were at risk, or executive image and financial rewards were in jeopardy. Executives would run around like chickens with their heads cut off, doing and saying whatever was needed to ensure their short-term objectives were achieved. Don't get me wrong; I was floating in the same boat. I wanted my bonus and stock incentives just as much as they did and knew very well that we all needed to succeed to survive.

Yet, there seemed to be a fundamental difference in our approach to the same reality; I was less concerned about political correctness or pleasing the boss, more willing to accept risk, and unwilling to alienate my team, which led me and my counterparts to draw very different lines in the sand.

And why wouldn't we? Our backgrounds and experiences were different. I relied on a strong supporting cast, straightforwardness, and clarity. Meanwhile, their self-reliance, ego, political sensitivities, career aspirations, and personal agendas caused them to approach life and business through a very different lens. My alternate approach often put me at odds with my counterparts and had me teetering on the fringes of the executive club.

Yet, my success rate, performance numbers, and employee engagement scores consistently surpassed my executive counterparts'. To me, this was validation that my atypical approach was the right one, and I stuck to it like white on rice.

It wasn't easy swimming against the current through shark-infested waters. Thankfully I was able to bob and weave my way through the clutter of egos and negative narratives, finding allies and always relying on my team. On occasion, I'd receive confirmation that I was doing the right thing, which was always appreciated. This type of validation was well expressed in a letter I received from a former employee almost two years after I retired:

Hi Rick,

Glad to hear you are doing well and putting your thoughts on leadership to paper. You've been gone a while now, but I wanted to pass along my thoughts on the impact you had on me and the team.

Over the span of a career, we all experience different leadership styles, and their effects cascade throughout a team. Those who have the privilege of experiencing different corporate cultures over the course of a career often seek to find an employee-centric workplace that promotes empowerment and value. While this may sound like common sense, and is heard in every corporate town hall, rarely do these values transition into practice. It's because of this disconnect that we see high levels of employment transitions.

My experience with you has had an impact on my career and has shaped my beliefs on the traits of truly great leaders. Exposure to senior leaders is often limited, but oddly enough, you were accessible to all levels of the team. This trait is common among leaders with high-performing units and high employee satisfaction scores. Your ability to connect with each member of RBG with genuine interest-inspired performance [and] your presence was a gift to the team, something that only exists in leaders who understand their people.

You consistently worked with your management team to remove barriers and drive performance. Empowerment is the key to success when you have a team of experts in your midst. Even during the most pressing projects, you could expect direct support and understanding. Our team cared because you did.

Context aside, the traits and style of your leadership are rare. Your ability to inspire, connect, and deliver is truly missed by the team. As my career continues to develop, working alongside someone of your caliber became far more important than title or compensation.

Thanks, for being you!

James Lavis

James's words certainly make me blush a little, but they capture much of what I've been talking about. I believe his assertion that my traits and leadership style was "rare" is, I believe, only a result of my profile being different from the typical people that companies promote into leadership positions. Companies are just looking in all the wrong places.

Determined to succeed

I was lucky to get the jobs I did. Having only worked for two companies, I was a known entity, which allowed me to get on the inside track, and typically I didn't have to take a test! When I interviewed for McKesson, I was lucky to know the company's former director and recruiter. When I moved through the executive ranks, three of my bosses, people with whom I had strong relationships, all went on to become president of the company.

So, let's face it, if it hadn't been for this good fortune, my profile, style, testing results, and lack of interviewing ability or executive flare would have killed any chance I had of getting those jobs. On top of that, I spent a career defending my approach and standing up for my team as corporate VPs and SVPs downplayed and even criticized our success.

They would tell us how lucky we were to have 'easy' customers, employees, and unions when the reality was that we knew how to deal with these people and groups, regardless of how difficult they might have been.

For example, when we convinced Pharmachoice to reverse their decision and remain with McKesson, they called us 'street fighters' and remarked, "Yeah, we need them in the company too," and then reneged on our bonuses.

When we pulled off the IDSC miracle, they tried to send in the smart people to get it done right while reducing my performance rating for standing up against corporate bullying. When we recruited twenty PSV stores for McKesson—a key factor in Pharmasave returning to

McKesson—we were criticized for interfering with the banner, and they told us "to mind your own business." When the contract with Sobeys finally got signed, the fact that we had brought that relationship back from the dead was oddly forgotten.

It was an endless list of hypocritical contradictions; we consistently drove the company's success and profitability, yet we were criticized by most executives for not following protocol. It seemed that regardless of how effective I was at bringing in financial results and building team engagement (the actual words in the mission statement), I was never seen as a leader by this group of executives. To them, I lacked a certain polish, style, and—my favorite—executive flare!

I never heard these leadership characteristics discussed at corporate meetings. Yet, they were the unwritten passcodes to the executive club. It was only when I started reporting directly to decision-makers that my approach became 'acceptable,' and my career path accelerated.

When these decision-makers got to watch us up close, experienced our culture firsthand, and saw the effectiveness of our operating style and our team's drive to achieve goals, then they finally got it.

Over the next three years, the Retail Banner Group would grow from 1,200 to 2,500 stores, organically growing by up to 300 individual independent pharmacies in a single year while successfully integrating larger groups like RemedyRx and Uniprix.

Our bottom line rapidly expanded (even as government legislation hammered our margins), turning us into a bigger and then the biggest contributor to McKesson Canada's bottom line. We built a world-class

Shared Service Organization, which brought leading-edge tools and processes to six banners and 2,500 stores, while our profit contribution grew exponentially.

All the while, we stayed focused on our employees, creating an environment where team members felt empowered and engaged. In an independently tabulated employee survey (used by thousands of the largest companies around the world), the Retail Banner Group scored twelve points higher than McKesson Canada and McKesson U.S., reaching the 'global best average' level! This meant that if you took the top employee survey results in the world across all companies, industries, and sectors and calculated their average score, we were performing at that high level! This was an amazing result, which demonstrated for the umpteenth time that superior performance and high levels of employee engagement are directly connected.

Understanding what kind of leader you want to be and how you define leadership will be fundamental to the type of leader you will become.

Don't be fooled into being something you're not; abandoning your values and skills will only serve to nullify your advantage and restrict your abilities. It's like giving an artist a hammer and asking them to build a house. The job will be done poorly; they will be reprimanded for underperforming and will never be promoted—as a carpenter, something they never wanted to be in the first place. I would urge you to stay strong and stick with the skills you know and value.

The ultimate showdown: Leader vs. Executive

I believe that there's a long list of differences between a leader and an executive. That's not to say that the two can't reside in the same person, but for all the reasons I have discussed, that's rather unlikely in the current scenario at most companies.

Regardless of all of our differences, I managed to play in the same sandbox with my executive colleagues, generally adhering to a code of conduct that kept us within an acceptable range of appropriateness.

That was soon to change, however, as I was about to encounter another type of executive: slicker, smoother, and more cunning. Someone who liked to play almost entirely outside the sandbox, with a hidden agenda wrapped up in chaos, confusion, and deceit.

Key takeaways

- Don't let your actions be driven by short-term goals and incentives.
- Always be honest and upfront with your team.
- A strong team does not diminish your individuality.

LESSON 21

Don't lose yourself in the madness

The ostrich is not hiding its head in the sand; it's showing you its ass.

Old Brennan wive's tale

In 2015, McKesson announced the creation of a CEO role in the Canadian marketplace to oversee its Canadian operations and the newly acquired Rexall Pharmacy Group. The CEO of choice was well-known to most of the Canadian Senior Management team, having been President of McKesson a decade earlier. Although he had been gone from McKesson for some time, he had maintained strong relationships with a number of the key players in the U.S., and with the acquisition of Rexall, they saw him as the perfect fit.

He had a reputation as a big thinker who had hundreds of projects running simultaneously. This typically resulted in competing mandates and a serious lack of accountability, which led his previous direct reports to have grave concerns about his return. Before he officially came on board, we all went to supper, and he told us about his sailing adventures around the world and why he was "giving it all up in the hope of effecting positive change in the Canadian health system."

To my surprise, many of my colleagues were rolling their eyes as he made his little speech. They later cautioned me to take what I had heard with a grain of salt and warned me against agreeing to too much too quickly. Essentially, in their experience, the man's words rarely matched his actions, and there was always a hidden agenda lurking in the shadows.

Ironically, these were the very same executives who always had ulterior motives of their own when I struggled with them over the years. I thought they had mastered the ups and downs of the executive world and its colourful characters, but despite their experience, they saw him as an entirely different beast.

Then, to everyone's surprise, Alain, our President, resigned. Undoubtedly, he did not want to deal with the CEO's management style all over again.

To put our new company leader's vision of health care into context, it was nothing new. It was what one could read in most trade magazines about the need to improve health care through digital tools, innovation, hybrid public-private initiatives, and one-stop health care—that kind of thing. Much of what he was suggesting was already part of our Retail Banner Group's strategic plan.

Unfortunately for me, staying clear of him was almost impossible. My Retail Banner business was directly in the line of fire, with the CEO's focus firmly on the newly acquired Rexall Pharmacy Group.

Trying to be a good corporate citizen

In good faith, I had my team take him through every program we had developed as well as our current initiatives. The magnitude and scale of what the team had accomplished seemed to blow him away.

At this point, we were getting along famously, and I was feeling pretty good about the future. Yet, this is where our formal collaboration ended.

Per the operating guidelines imposed on McKesson by the Competition Board of Canada, McKesson Canada (including my group) and Rexall Pharmacies could not share information, work together, or communicate in any way. Only the CEO could work with both McKesson Canada and Rexall, but he, too, could not share information. Sound crazy? It was!

So, when it came to engineering the Rexall turnaround, the ball was firmly in the CEO's court. Rexall's financial performance was well below expectations, and as my fellow executives explained, the real reason he was hired was to ensure the company got its anticipated financial return on its $3 billion investment. More importantly, his performance targets and compensation package would be directly tied to Rexall's performance.

Truth be told

Knowing our new CEO as they did, my peers knew that he'd do everything in his power to meet those expectations.

Over many months, his style would emerge, as predicted. He was slick, smooth-talking, and, on the surface, a very likable guy. His operational mantra was, "Let's try everything and see what works."

This may sound cool, but with no added employees, it only led to people being overworked and running in different directions, with little understanding of what was really important.

To formalize his plan, he enlisted the help of a consulting group, to which he gave his predetermined vision. We were supposed to believe they were working for free. Next, he built his team, which consisted of loyal past executives, old-school thinkers, and young MBAs, not one of whom had any retail pharmacy experience.

As his team and the consultants got down to business, confusion and disarray soon followed. The consultants seemed to be solely focused on validating the CEO's assumptions rather than developing a fact-based plan with input from the business unit.

His executive team ran amok, inserting their opinions and using the authority of the CEO's office to pressure my team into altering timelines and directives. Their mandates seemed counterintuitive to our collective success. His team and ours were working in opposing directions; they were developing programs in isolation and duplicating existing programs.

My executive peers were also frustrated with his nonsensical interference, but they seemed more resigned to the new reality and went into self-protection mode. I was in the direct line of fire and had no choice but to address the issues. So, I organized a meeting with my boss (the president) and the CEO.

When the time came for our three-way meeting, the CEO used some creative math to demonstrate that the growth of Corporate Pharmacy and the entrance of the Amazon online pharmacy into the Canadian market (which was not really in sight) would kill independent pharmacies within a few years.

Regardless of how much I might have wanted to agree with him and get back into his good graces, his characterizations of the facts were just plain silly. I just couldn't buy in.

I tried to offer him a plan that would allow both groups to prosper, but that wasn't what he wanted to hear. So, we all left the meeting, and subsequent meetings, frustrated.

What I couldn't understand was why he was prepared to put the Retail Banner Group's profit bucket at risk. After all, it was a major piece of McKesson Canada's profits. It made no sense; something else had to be more important!

Based on these meetings and his team's actions over the course of several months, it became clear that the expansion of the Corporate Pharmacy business was at the core of his plan, and the growing strength of the independent business was an obstacle to his objectives.

Then, things started to happen, quietly at first. Budget dollars seemed to get reallocated, IT resources were pulled, and revenues were reassigned, making it incredibly difficult for my team to complete our projects or achieve our financial objectives.

Soon, the negative narrative started to pick up. The CEO and his SVPs accused me and my team of creating programs without approval and being uncooperative. They even went as far as suggesting that my team was unhappy with my leadership.

While all this was going on, Corporate USA decided to do a major evaluation of its business structure, looking for ways to consolidate and leverage the company's business assets around the world.

I was asked to participate in a committee that would look at the potential of centralizing McKesson's Independent Pharmacy infrastructure within North America, which included RBG and the Health Mart chain in the U.S. Guided by a consultant hired by McKesson Corp., we created a working group that included executives from the various North American retail pharmacy organizations. The committee unanimously agreed that a North American Shared Service center could be created and operated out of our office in Toronto, leveraging the existing Canadian infrastructure.

When our recommendation went to the McKesson Corp. Executive Steering Committee (our CEO included) for approval, we received no acknowledgment. Nothing! Not a rejection, not an acceptance, just freaking crickets!

When I questioned what was going on, I was told by way of the CEO that a key player in the U.S. was upset and unsupportive of our recommendations. In response to this 'revelation,' Shawn, our president, and I individually spoke to the executive in question to understand his concerns. He had no recollection of any such conversation with the CEO.

Coming to terms with reality

The whole sequence of events played out like a bad TV drama with bad actors and a poorly written script. Even when we surpassed our financial expectations, disproved every negative characterization (in writing), increased our store count by three hundred independent locations, and scored Global Best Average on our employee engagement survey (twelve points higher than the rest of the company), they still refused to acknowledge our accomplishments.

It was mentally exhausting!

I remember talking to my wife about it. I was so frustrated and felt like a total failure, and then it hit me: What was going on had nothing to do with me! I was simply an obstacle, blocking him from achieving his objectives. In his mind, I was no more than collateral damage. I can't say this realization made me feel any better, but it did allow me to come to terms with the proverbial writing on the wall. I regained my sense of self and changed my game plan; I went from worrying about what he thought to pivoting toward an exit strategy.

As I reflected on the events of that last year, I couldn't help but marvel at how quickly our environment had deteriorated and how one person (with authority) could kill a culture that had taken years to build.

The company you keep

It was pretty clear that my approach to leadership and our CEO's couldn't be further apart. While my limitations inspired me to evolve and surround myself with people who were *'more* than myself,' who brought skills and perspectives that I lacked, he surrounded himself with people who he saw as *less* than himself—men and women who believed in the wisdom of authority and obedience to rules, the kind of people who would unconditionally buy into his vision and operating style.

As I pondered the mayhem of the previous several months, it became clear that my straightforward style, disciplined operating approach, and unwavering support of my team and the facts must have almost driven him mad. Good for me—ha!

Little did he know that as an 'atypical,' life had taught me to stick to what worked for me, to be proud of my unique skill set, and to never be bullied into believing that wrong was right.

Although my departure took place sooner than I had planned, I felt good about my decision. I moved on knowing that you can't win 'em all. The best team doesn't always win, nor does the best leader always end up on top.

Sometimes, you have to come to terms with reality, as shitty as it might be. Other times, you just have to go down a different path and find a better team with an operating style compatible with yours and values more like your own.

In my case, considering my age, my personal circumstances, and my relaxed financial situation, I picked retirement.

My choice, however, doesn't mean I didn't enjoy the last laugh. There was an obvious storm on the horizon, and I had jumped ship in the nick of time. Essentially, Independent Pharmacy continued to flourish in Canada, and most of the CEO's 'big' ideas never left the drawing board. His disruptive executives were fired, employee engagement numbers plummeted, and many of my CET colleagues ended up leaving the company. Quite a master class in leadership!

Key takeaways

- Changing who you are to please the boss is a fool's game.
- Sticking to what you believe in can be very uncomfortable at times but is nonetheless required.

LESSON 22

Understanding the atypical leader's headspace

When your efforts run in the face of conventional wisdom and accepted mastery, persistence can look like madness.

Hilary Austen

As I moved closer to retirement, I couldn't help but reflect on my life and career. I felt good about my accomplishments. It was clear that I had reached a level of success that most would have thought impossible for a guy like me.

Still, the negative experiences during my last months with the company consumed my every thought. It was like my brain was on this continuous loop. The pressure to conform, the negative environment, and the misleading narratives had pushed me to almost believe that I was incapable and unworthy of my position.

As an 'atypical,' and as a result of a lifetime of struggles and internal conflicts, embedded in my psyche was this underlying belief that I wasn't good enough, that my accomplishments were somehow just a fluke, and that the executive charade that I had managed to pull off would be uncovered at any moment.

Yet, the more practical side of my brain remained logical and confident. I had an unwavering determination to stick to my way of doing things, regardless of how much crap they slung my way.

Unfortunately, that didn't stop the torture of consistently rehashing every event in my mind a thousand times, but I knew that was just me and the way my brain worked, so I learned to live with it.

In the end, it didn't matter what was going on in my head or what those insufferable executives said or did. My determination, coupled with years of experience dealing with executive dysfunction, misleading narratives, and an understanding of my internal triggers, allowed me to cope and remain strong.

It was also during this time that I started to receive letters and phone calls of appreciation from past and present team members. Their comments clearly supported my way of doing things—my 'done is better than perfect' approach, the 'dog with a bone' mindset, and my ability to cut through the crap and shoot from the hip. Interestingly, these were the very same qualities that seemed to send the CEO and his band of merry fellows into spasms.

As I pondered over this antagonistic take on my style, it reconfirmed in my mind that the way I spoke, operated, and formulated my thinking was just a case of me being me. I had to use the most basic of approaches; my perspective was people-based and grounded in common-sense and real-world scenarios. Resorting to simplification, clear language, and strong organization was the only way I could get anything done.

Embrace what makes you different

If you are an 'atypical,' I encourage you to embrace your differences. There are many studies of how people with so-called 'invisible disabilities' behave in the workplace. Most efforts by 'atypicals,' it seems, go into concealing their differences.

In my career, although I often hid my shortcomings, I found that opening up about my so-called hidden disabilities was crucial in several key moments. If I hadn't explained what I knew about myself to recruiters, psychologists, and certain bosses, I would probably never have made it to the top ranks of McKesson.

Researchers from the Center for Talent Innovation (CTI) have found that about a third of white-collar professionals in the United States have a disability, yet only one in ten of them disclose it to their employers. That means that companies are missing out on understanding how the atypical brain can potentially benefit and contribute to a company's success.

According to Lisa Baird and Victoria Reese, two of the top researchers in the field, "People with disabilities may bring special skills, finely honed skills, or a fierce drive that makes them uniquely valuable to organizations." I want you to mark these words because I am, again, living proof of that statement's veracity. Instead of hiding your uniqueness, understand and harness its powers. It should drive you to achieve more than most.

Don't take my word for it; listen to the people who have been out in the field researching this stuff. According to Julia Taylor Kennedy, a CTI spokesperson, interviews and focus groups reveal that "people with disabilities are particularly innovative. In order to navigate the world with a disability, they have to problem-solve each day."

According to a landmark report on the topic, "Leaders with disabilities who have risen to the tops of their organizations may have unique leadership qualities relative to other leaders." Ring any bells?

Auto-theory, a term used by Paul B. Preciado, Lauren Fournier, and other modern thinkers, refers to writing that integrates autobiography "and other explicitly subjective and embodied modes with discourses of philosophy and theory."

I have only now understood that this is what I have been doing: creating my own theories based on my lived experiences. There was virtually no literature about being a business leader as an 'atypical' that I could refer to when I began my journey. I had to make my own way. It hasn't been easy, but it has also been an incredibly rewarding process.

There is no such thing as normal

In the first chapter, I shared messages I received from three different people, but not because those individuals were my biggest cheerleaders or my closest friends. Quite the opposite, the first two notes were from two guys with whom I had had countless arguments. I bet they struggled to appreciate my leadership style over the years, yet somehow, their frustrations eventually turned into appreciation.

I had no idea how these people felt. I don't recall any 'aha' moments, special favors, or especially meaningful interactions. All I remember is that we worked together in what I thought was a normal environment. Yet, I guess what they told me in those letters was that our 'normal' wasn't so normal after all!

This brought me to the next important question: Is there such a thing as normal? We are all unique in our own ways, and we deal with our stuff using the perspective and skills we've accumulated based on our experiences. The system, on the other hand, keeps trying to put us into the same box, making us adapt to a single set of rules. It's almost as if acting the same way could make us think the same way. I have learned the hard way that this is not the case

I believe that if we want to get the most out of individuals, teams, and leaders, it would be more beneficial to match people with others who can balance their shortcomings with their strengths and enhance their skill sets—the makings of a team.

All too often, I saw how Corporate HR matched candidates to the words on a job description and a predetermined personality profile, with almost no regard for the applicant's personality, strengths, and weaknesses. There seemed to be this failure to recognize that a 'company' is a collection of individuals organized into a team led by managers with varying styles and skills.

For me, it was a matter of survival. Conforming to the wisdom of the system or adapting to someone else's version of what I should be would have been the end of me. I made it a point to hire people who made me and the team better. If that meant fighting with HR, debating with my boss, or circumventing a few rules, then that's what I did.

My approach didn't always make me Mr. Popular with the corporate establishment, and I was okay with that. I sought out allies when I needed them and learned to back off and let it go when I could see I was going too far.

As you can imagine, in terms of talent composition and psychological makeup, my teams were very different from others. As a result, they looked, acted, and performed quite differently from the rest—just what I was hoping for.

As my retirement date approached, the company held the proverbial retirement parties. The Retail Banner staff hosted a reception in the lobby of our building. Lunch was served; speeches were made; people thanked me for my time; we had cake. It was nice; it felt right.

The next party, hosted by my management group, forced me to do the 'Skywalk' around the top of Toronto's 1,815-foot CN Tower alongside ten of my RBG team members. It was terrifying! The edge walk was followed by a lovely supper. We were joined by McKesson executives from various business units who I had worked with over the years. Gifts were given, speeches made, we had cake. . . Again, it felt right!

My fake team

These two events were what you'd expect to see when a well-known executive retires. There were two more events that better illustrate the difference between what a team should be and what it often is.

To recognize my retirement, the CET invited me to join them for supper in Montreal. Don't forget that I had often been reminded that the

CET was my real team, so I was on the edge of my seat with anticipation ahead of our final hoorah.

We all met for a drink at the hotel bar before going to supper, where a toast was made in my honor. I received a couple of corporate-funded gifts: a picture and a jersey of Alex Galchenyuk, a Montreal Canadiens player. The funny thing was that I already owned an Alex Galchenyuk jersey, which I had worn on many occasions. Oh, well, now I had two.

When the drinks were done and it was time to go to the restaurant, I asked the group to give me a couple of minutes to toss the gifts into my room. It took three minutes, tops! When I returned to the lobby, it was empty. I couldn't find anyone; had they all left?

There I was, standing in the lobby like a discombobulated wet noodle, standing alone without a clue where to go for my fringe retirement party.

By sheer chance, an executive assistant came along and rescued me. He ordered me a cab, I gave him the address, and off I went to my party!

When I arrived at the restaurant, I thought they'd be apologetic, but nope! They hadn't even noticed I wasn't there! Disappointing, yes, but then I figured that once I took my distinguished seat of honor in the middle of the table, the spotlight would turn to me. But, to my surprise, the only seat open was tucked away at the far end of the long, twenty-person table. After some time, Paula pointed out to the rest of the group that I should be sitting in the middle. Everyone nodded in agreement, and then they went right back to their drinks. Nobody did anything!

After dinner, I went back to the hotel, stuffed with food yet void of any special feeling and laughing to myself about my 'heartfelt' retirement supper. The next morning, I was headed out of the hotel to catch my flight when I ran into our SVP of Communications in the elevator. To add insult to injury, instead of just saying "have a good flight," he said, "I'll give you a call in a couple of days to chat, and we'll get together." I knew that would never happen, and it never did.

Oh, and by the way, Montreal traded Alex Galchenyuk the next day (an omen?), so my duplicate jersey became even more useless. After this anticlimax of an homage, I couldn't pack my bags fast enough and headed back to New Brunswick.

The wonders of a true team

A few weeks later, Guy and Sheldon from McKesson Atlantic invited me and my buddy Rod out for a round of golf. After the round, I invited them to my place for a drink, and they obliged. As I headed home and turned onto my street, I could see a group of people blocking the road. I wondered what the hell was going on. As I got closer, I realized it was the McKesson Atlantic team waving signs and holding up a banner, yelling and screaming, *"Happy Retirement!"* As I drove up to my house, the front lawn was crowded; it was the rest of the Atlantic team, plus the MacIntyres, McDonoughs, Whites, Ringette families, neighbors, and friends. Even Morgan, my son, had flown in from Toronto!

As I moved toward 'Rick's Café,' I couldn't believe my eyes! Shawn, Melita, Paula S., Joanne, and Melanie from the RBG group were all there. They had all flown in from Toronto at their own expense. And they came with a special gift: a kick-ass karaoke machine. Monique (the 'Noise Nazi') would hate them forever, but we would worry about that later.

Then, there she was, live and in full color: Joanne LeBlanc from back in my early Shoppers days. She hadn't changed a bit! As the night carried on, speeches were made, we reminisced about the old times, and Shirley and the IDSC girls wrote and sang a song about our misadventures together. The karaoke machine got a full workout, and we danced and partied well into the wee hours.

With all the excitement and so many good friends in one place, I couldn't help but get lost in the moment, and I swung into full party mode. I may have scared the Toronto ladies a little—ha! The Atlantic group dragged themselves home late that night. Meanwhile, the Toronto crowd stayed the night at the cottage, and we were able to properly say our goodbyes in the morning.

I found out that night that many Atlantic team members wanted to attend one of the retirement parties held in Toronto but were told by management that they were not allowed. So, they decided to put on their own non-company-sponsored event.

That night was amazing! I felt incredibly appreciated. I was so humbled by my former teams' efforts to say goodbye to me in style, and their words left me speechless:

"You made us smile!"

"Your positive energy was contagious!"

"You made us feel important!"

"You taught us to take time to enjoy life!"

"Most importantly, you were a true leader, mentor, and coach."

"Done is better than perfect, baby!"

My experiences with these two different groups were diametrically opposed. On the one hand, there were the people I managed who understood and supported me unconditionally; on the other hand, there were the executives, so consumed by their agendas and self-importance that I was invisible to them. That doesn't mean they weren't nice people or that I didn't have friends on the CET; I did. But that in itself didn't alter the fact that as a 'team,' we ran on empty.

Despite the CET's irreverence and the CEO's antics, I felt like I'd had a great and satisfying career. I worked for two solid companies, had loads of fun, met lots of great people, and lived a pretty good career life. And the positive comments I received gave me a strong sense of validation. To walk away knowing that I had such a positive impact on so many people is beyond any words I'm capable of writing!

Key takeaways

- If I've learned anything, it's to embrace your imperfections.
- Being part of a high-functioning team is an amazing, life-altering experience.

Final reflections

Find out who you are, and do it on purpose.

Dolly Parton

As I reflect on my executive years, I must admit that I feel an immense amount of pride in both my personal growth and the level I reached in the corporate ranks. The feedback I received from my team, my industry-leading employee engagement scores, and my business unit's success seem to validate that I did become a leader, after all. Against all odds!

Yet, the feeling of accomplishment goes far beyond career accolades. I didn't reinvent the pizza delivery model, create Facebook, or become a global CEO. My story isn't one of accomplishing the impossible and changing the world. It's my account of accomplishing what, to me, felt impossible and, in the process, changed my life. Coming from my shit-filled, slow-class, drunk and high, humble beginnings to miraculously find my place atop a global pharmaceutical conglomerate, I'd say that was something to be proud of.

So, yes, the achievements felt gratifying, the titles were validating, and everything I learned along the way was invaluable. But what really filled me with pride was knowing that I did it my way, unapologetically—that I tore through the bullshit labels forced on me and dismantled the notion that I needed to fit inside a predetermined box of competencies to become successful.

It's been a long, imperfect journey. It took me years to find my way and understand who the hell I even was—to figure out what I had to offer and how to get organized and gain the confidence to just be me. My style was my own—albeit flawed, ass-backward, and misguided at times. Take it or leave it, like it or hate it, I didn't let go of myself.

Let me tell you, though, it got ugly at times. I was pissing in the wind for years. But sure enough, slowly and steadily, my skills emerged, like a blind person whose disability enhances their other senses. I became a master of organization, clarity, simplicity, and delegation. I instinctively knew I couldn't do it alone, so surrounding myself with the right people was at the core of my strategy.

My approach was undoubtedly self-serving in the beginning, but as time passed, I came to recognize that being part of a highly functioning and motivated team made me greater than the sum of my parts. That certainly doesn't mean that everyone I encountered thought I was a leader and agreed with my decision-making. I pissed off legions of people and acted like a dumbass on more than one occasion. It was all part of the process.

More than anything, it became clear to me that it's our imperfections that draw us to one another and help us form meaningful relationships. There is undeniable authenticity in both embracing and sharing your shortcomings. In the same way, there is deception inherent in hiding them.

It's my belief that the corporate façade, the stiff suits and fake smiles, are what often hinder true connections the most. I don't think anyone has ever built a deep, meaningful relationship because someone spoke perfect English, dressed impeccably, or knew where to put the soup spoon. No, it's the guy who can't dance but does it anyway, the teammate who loses their cool but can laugh about it, or the unrelenting best friend who refuses to let a few bullets and an expired passport ruin his good time. So, look for those you connect with, those who share your values and know what's important in life. Find your tribe and buy them a beer.

As you can imagine, people like me, those with learning disabilities and mediocre writing skills, don't publish a ton of books. As a result, our unique perspective is rarely acknowledged or considered in the leadership discussion, which will hopefully change now.

The science behind atypicals: neurodiversity

A high-level HR professional recently explained to me that there's a new concept coming into vogue in the business world called neurodiversity. Which helps supports my story and explain the gifts that I was able to discover within my perceived limitations.

Neurodiversity is a term applied to people with diagnosed or undiagnosed neurological deviations from the norm, including dyslexia, cognitive dysfunction, anxiety disorders, OCD, ADHD, and conditions that fall on the autism spectrum. It refers to the variations in the human brain and cognition, such as in terms of sociability, learning, attention, mood, and other mental functions.

The concept of neurodiversity celebrates these differences as valuable variations and an important part of human diversity—something to be celebrated, not cured.[11]

The people I described as 'atypical' are the undiagnosed individuals who don't fall solely into one particular neurological condition but overlap on to one another. Each person is different, each with their own unique cocktail of limitations and corresponding skills, abilities, and perspectives.

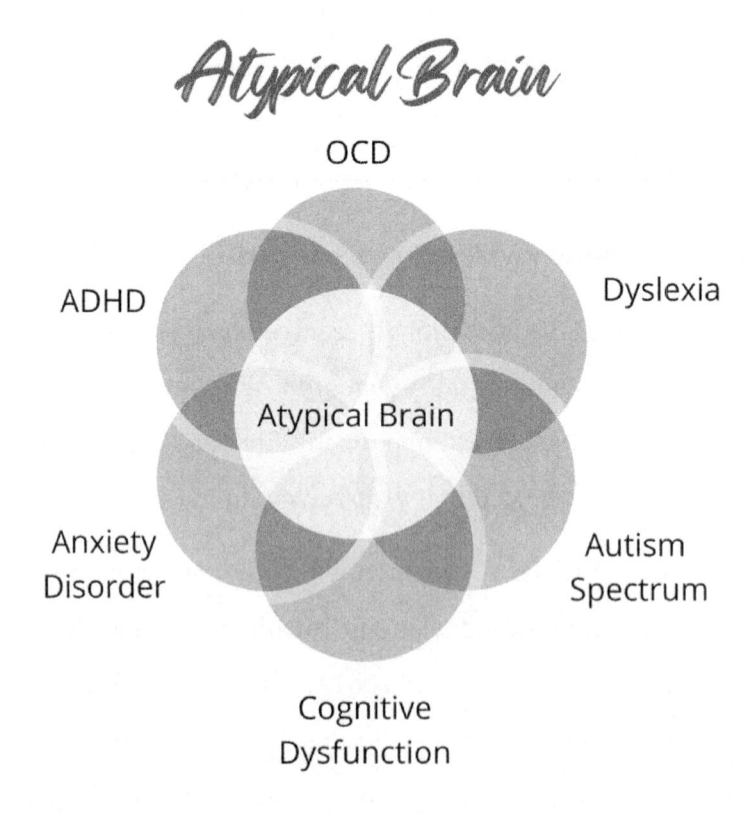

Atypical Brain

OCD

ADHD

Dyslexia

Atypical Brain

Anxiety Disorder

Autism Spectrum

Cognitive Dysfunction

With this new appreciation and understanding of neurodiversity on the rise, I am hopeful that society and the business world will begin to better understand and maximize the potential of the Atypical brain and people on the Neurodivse spectrum.

To make this book come to life as a neurodiverse person, I spent countless hours juggling words, trying to make the pieces fit, and finding people to help me tell my story. Writing it has been a transcendental experience filled with self-reflection. I'm living proof that your perceived faults, disabilities, and missteps don't define who you are, and that within each of us lies a path to success through self-discovery.

This applies to all of us, regardless of our stories, identities, and whatever circumstances we've had to overcome. Find the power within you, celebrate your uniqueness, and unleash your atypical superpowers on the world—and to hell with what the neighbors think!

Bonus: How to get started

Complexity is the enemy of execution.

Tony Robbins

As I've come to the end of my story, I've been asked by numerous people to include a final section that might organize the twenty-two lessons and the many takeaways into a simple actionable plan.

Here's my four-step action plan:

Step 1: Know who you are.

Step 2: Create the right environment.

Step 3: Get organized.

Step 4: Take action.

Step One: Know who you are

We're all different, with different skills and perspectives based on where our atypical brain overlaps on the neurodiversity spectrum, and it is this very uniqueness that gives all of us a particular and singular set of skills. Understanding who you are critical to your future success.

Seven ways to get to know the real you

- Consult your trusted friends and colleagues, and talk to people who you believe to be positive role models, regardless of their position or status.

- Get tested outside of work by professionals; find out where your atypical brain lies on the neurodiversity spectrum.
- Get out into the non-business world to gain perspective.
- Take a personal inventory of your strengths and weaknesses, then compare them to what your friends, colleagues, and professionals say (be honest with yourself).
- Commit to your natural skills, unique perspective, and values.
- Look for help when you need it; remember that asking for help is a display of confidence.
- Be unafraid to be you.

Let's assume that you've done a good job understanding your limitations, strengths, and weaknesses. Congratulations! However, embracing this new version of you for all to see is quite another thing.

Bosses and managers will tell you, using logic and rationality, why your approach doesn't work and how toeing the company line and conforming to the status quo will better advance your career. In the short term, they might be right. However, this approach will suck the life out of you, robbing you of the joy of work and preventing you from reaching your true potential.

Maximize your unique potential

- Embrace your weirdness and use your regrets to fuel positive change.
- Realize that making mistakes is how you learn.
- Accept and laugh at your blunders.
- Stop trying to be everything to everybody.

- Understand that your perception of leadership will have everything to do with the leader you will become—so get it right.
- Pick your friends carefully; they will have everything to do with who you will become.
- Know that twisting and contorting yourself into something you are not will only make you less effective.

Develop traits that will enhance your gifts

- Become self-aware.
- Learn to be humble.
- Take courses and seminars that will neutralize your weaknesses.
- Master your strengths.
- Incorporate your strengths into your daily activities.
- Eliminate wasted time.
- Become comfortable taking risks (get comfortable, be uncomfortable).
- Reject complexity at every turn.
- Learn to value people.

Step Two: Create an environment where you and your team can shine

Once you understand how your brain works, you will need to commit to your particular set of skills and perspectives and find an environment that allows you to be at your best. An environment where you feel relaxed, accepted, and supported will allow your brain function to improve and your anxiety to diminish.

Your environment needs to be:

- People-centered (defined by what they do and not by what they say)
- Where colleagues take pride in helping one another
- Devoid of façades; conversations are simple, clear, and straightforward
- Where relationships are easy to build
- Where you love to go every day
- Where everyone is equally accountable
- Where it's frigging fun

Becoming a high-performance team

The characteristics of high-performing teams (HPTs) are a secret to no one. They are discussed ad nauseam in countless leadership books and presented at scads of seminars. Yet, they rarely come to life. Current managerial profiles, pressure to meet short-term objectives, bureaucracy, HR policies, and political agendas stifle team dynamics and never allow HPTs to take flight. You need to take a different approach, prioritizing actions over words and values over personal agenda. Your goal should be to create the conditions where your team can become greater than the sum of its parts—a place where the joy of work and the pride of doing a good job ooze out of every team member's pores.

High-performance team basics

- Explain your expectations to the team, not just about performance but about what the right attitude looks like. You'll get some giggles, but that's okay. Stick to your guns.
- Reorganize: Identify roles, duties, and timelines in detail, leaving no room for misinterpretation.
- Be clear on what accountability means and how you will manage underperformance.
- Listen to what's being said around you.
- Get employees focused on their jobs, and minimize distractions.
- Get your team out of meetings and off needless calls.
- Hire attitude first, skills second.
- Be honest and bold in your expectations.
- Deal with issues immediately and consistently.
- And, yes, terminate employees who refuse to adapt.

Critical to developing a high-performance team is creating time, or at least not wasting it. There are only so many hours in the day, and you need to use them wisely.

Creating time

- Only participate in meetings and calls that are relevant to you and your business.
- Do not attend meetings or calls simply because you were invited; politely decline.
- If you must go to a meeting, coordinate with your teammates, and avoid sending multiple team members.

- Don't read every email; look at the title and author and decide if it's relevant.
- Say what needs to be said; don't waste time with political nonsense.
- Keep things simple; remember that complexity is the enemy.
- Everyone on the team must be held to the same level of performance.
- Balance transparency and good sense.

The secret sauce

- Hard work and fun should coexist.
- Find ways to have fun outside of work.
- Find humor in difficult situations.
- Allow coworkers to have fun disagreeing with you.
- Allow each individual to be their own unique self.
- Don't act humble; be humble.
- Do what you say, and if you can't or don't, explain why.
- Real learning is the result of doing; stop talking about it.

Remember that:

- Stubbornness and persistence can be virtues.
- Rules stifle creativity.
- Good ideas are more likely to come to you when you're cutting the lawn (or when you're engaged in almost any other activity) than in meetings.
- Boundaries are just choices.
- There is so much more to you that you could never fit into a box.

Step Three: Organization

Throughout my career, simplicity, clarity, organization, reliance on people, and a dogmatic approach to achieving my goals were the cornerstones of my management style, and my teams loved it.

I was so stubborn and fixated on reaching my goals that I couldn't help but explore every possibility from every angle, over and over, until I found a path forward—even if that meant pissing off my colleagues or shaking up the status quo.

But make no mistake. Whichever path I took, basic organization was fundamental to our success. Getting everyone on the same page and moving in the same direction was critical. It's what set us apart from the crowd.

Setting the Stage

- Job descriptions are a must, but they usually fall short of clarifying day-to-day activities.
- Employees should create their own detailed job schedules with timelines and then share them with management and the rest of the team.
- Understanding individual accountability is essential to maximizing performance; be clear and straightforward.
- Follow-up with employees is an art form. Don't do it so often that you minimize their sense of ownership or so seldom that they'll head off in the wrong direction.
- If you want people to take risks, let them make mistakes.
- Use the 'done is better than perfect' (DIBTP) philosophy.

DIBTP philosophy

. Keeping it simple is at the core of the DIBTP strategy. Break projects into phases, avoiding the bells and whistles in the initial phases. Then, divide the phases into sections, the sections into components, the components into tasks, and the tasks into small doable pieces. Dig deep into the operational guts of every component, ensuring that everyone on the team understands the tasks at hand, their role, everyone else's role, and how they are interconnected.

As a manager, listen to the conversations, challenge colleagues' understanding, observe the body language, and only let the discussion end when you see the proverbial light bulb go on for every single team member. These detailed discussions are critical to establishing accountability and ensuring that each team member understands how their efforts fit into the big picture.

If you've been successful in creating the right environment, people will speak up, ask for help, challenge you, and look for clarity (if they don't, go back to Step Two). Stay in perpetual motion, learn as you go, fix things on the fly, and don't let the unknown or a conservative mindset bring the team to a standstill.

Step Four: Take action

Remember that even the best-laid plans can come crashing down. Things change, situations evolve, and scads of people both internally and externally will have differing opinions on pretty much everything. Recognizing this reality and dealing with it with enthusiasm instead of frustration is an important piece in achieving success.

Stay the course

- Be committed to the DIBTP philosophy; don't be browbeaten into complexifying the process.
- Moving forward without all the answers is a necessary reality if you want to accomplish anything.
- Therefore, accepting risks is unavoidable if you want to accomplish anything.
- Understand that knowledge comes from doing, and if you never get started, you'll never learn.
- Keep your customers and teammates informed; don't wait for the next meeting to raise issues.
- Adjust your plan when necessary.
- Communicate and make your progression meetings meaningful. Review objectives, results, and timelines; identify problems; fix them; move forward; repeat.
- Ask for help.
- Balance transparency with partiality.
- Be like a dog with a bone.

Well, there you have it. Go out into the world and embrace who you are. Find an environment where you and your team can shine, get organized, and go make it happen. The magic of this step-by-step guide lies in simplicity.

References

[1] Alter, N. (2017). The stranger's gaze. In Chanlat, J.-F. and Özbilgin, M.F. (eds), *Management and Diversity: Thematic Approaches*. London: Emerald, pp. 87–105.

[2] Wiggins, T. (2019). *Disabled Leadership*.

[3] Tolle, E. (2001). The power of now. Hodder Paperback.

[4] Carnegie, D. (1964). How to win friends and influence people. New York: Simon and Schuster.

[5] Anderson, A. R., & Fowers, B. J. (2020). An exploratory study of friendship characteristics and their relations with hedonic and eudaimonic well-being. *Journal of Social and Personal Relationships, 37*(1), 260–280. https://doi.org/10.1177/0265407519861152

[6] *24 Entrepreneurs Share Ideas on How to Think Outside The Box*. Retrieved from: https://rescue.ceoblognation.com/2020/04/24/entrepreneurs-share-ideas-on-how-to-think-outside-the-box/

[7] *How to Grow Your Business by Thinking Outside the Box*. Retrieved from: www.inc.com/martin-zwilling/how-to-grow-your-business-by-thinking-outside-the-box.html

[8] *Supporting Students' Postsecondary Success Amid Pandemic Interruptions*. Retrieved from: www.forbes.com/sites/chuckswoboda/2020/08/03/why-thinking-outside-the-box-is-the-wrong-way-to-approach-innovation/?sh=4d4c1eb1461b

[9] *Overcoming a bias against risk*. Retrieved from: www.mckinsey.com/business-functions/strategy-and-corporate-finance/our-insights/overcoming-a-bias-against-risk

[10] Hamlet by William Shakespeare.

[11] *What is neurodiversity*. www.youtube.com/watch?v=8YHom6Xs0oQ

Printed in Great Britain
by Amazon